The Case Against the Common Law

The Case Against the Common Law

Gordon Tullock

Karl Eller Professor of Economics and Political Science
University of Arizona

Contributions by

Amanda J. Owens and
Charles K. Rowley

The Blackstone Commentaries, No. 1
Series Editor: Amanda J. Owens

CAROLINA ACADEMIC PRESS

Durham, North Carolina

ISBN 0-89089-958-4
LCCN 96-71343

Carolina Academic Press
700 Kent Street
Durham, NC 27701
Telephone (919) 489-7486
Fax (919) 493-5668

Printed in the United States of America.

The Locke Institute

Founded in 1989, The Locke Institute is an independent, non-partisan, educational and research organization. The Institute is named for John Locke (1632-1704), philosopher and political theorist, who based his theory of society on natural law which required that the ultimate source of political sovereignty was with the individual. Individuals are possessed of inalienable rights variously defined by Locke as "life, health, liberty and possession," or, more directly, "life, liberty and property." It is the function of the state to uphold these rights since individuals would not enter into a political society unless they believed it would protect their lives, liberties and properties.

The Locke Institute seeks to engender a greater understanding of the concept of natural rights, its implications for constitutional democracy and for economic organization in modern society. The Institute encourages high quality research utilizing in particular modern theories of property rights, public choice, law and economics, and the new institutional economics as a basis for a more profound understanding of important and controversial issues in political economy. To this end, it commissions books, monographs, and shorter studies involving substantive scholarship written for a wider audience, organizes major conferences on fundamental topics in political economy, and supports independent research.

In order to maintain independence, The Locke Institute accepts no government funding. Funding for the Institute is solicited from private foundations, corporations, and individuals. In addition, the Institute raises funds from the sale of publications and from conference fees. The Institute is incorporated in the State of Virginia,

USA, and enjoys non-profit, tax-exempt status under Section 501(c)(3) of the United States Internal Revenue Code.

Officers of the Institute are listed above. Please direct all inquiries to the address given below.

4084 University Drive, Suite 103, Fairfax, Virginia 22030
Tel. (703) 934 6960   Fax. (703) 352 9747

Contents

Preface

The *Blackstone Commentaries* were devised in 1996 to create a stream of authoritative, independent and lucid analyses of the law and legal systems from a classical liberal perspective. Named for William Blackstone, the famous late eighteenth century scholar of English law, whose *Commentaries on the Laws of England* (1783) stand even now as a landmark contribution to jurisprudence, the *Blackstone Commentaries* will feature the ideas of distinguished scholars on the working of the legal system.

As always, the views expressed in this monograph are those of the author, not *The Locke Institute* (which has no corporate view). However, both expert and lay observers will find great value in Gordon Tullock's penetrating critique of the United States common law system and in his review of criminal and civil law reforms.

March 1996

Amanda J. Owens
Director of Legal Studies
The Locke Institute

Acknowledgments

I am extremely grateful to Amanda J. Owens and Charles K. Rowley for making significant research contributions to this monograph and for providing very thorough and conscientious editorial support which has significantly improved the quality of the monograph. I am grateful to The Locke Institute, through the editorial direction of Amanda J. Owens, for introducing *The Blackstone Commentaries* which makes it possible for me to collate a body of scholarship on the law which has demanded much of my time since I first wrote on the subject in *The Logic of the Law* (1971). My thanks are also due to the Institute for its efficient secretarial services in connection with the typing and preparation of the manuscript. It gives me great pleasure to initiate *The Blackstone Commentaries* with this monograph.

1. Introduction

This monograph provides an unusually comprehensive critical evaluation of the common law—a term, like many other legal terms, that is ambiguous. As Posner (1992, 31) has noted, the common law is used to encompass: the body of principles applied by the royal courts of England in the eighteenth century; the fields of law that have been created largely by judges as the by-product of deciding cases, rather than by legislatures; or any other field of law shaped largely by judicial precedents. In this monograph, I shall concern myself primarily with the common law in the second sense outlined above, focusing primarily on the criminal law, the law of property, the law of contracts and the law of torts; branches of the law that many of my colleagues in the law and economics movement view as being economically efficient. As the reader readily will determine, I beg to differ with respect to this Panglossian rush to judgment.

The institutional principles both of common law and of civil law adjudication are grounded in the social functions of courts. Like other complex institutions, courts serve many functions. However, two of these are paramount (Eisenberg 1988). The first function concerns the resolution of disputes that derive from a claim of right based on the application, meaning, and implications of a society's existing standards. In the U.S. system, the resolution of such disputes is a central function of the courts. To this end, courts are structured to be passive, acting only when set in motion by a party with a claim. Similarly, courts are limited to actions that are responsive to the actionable claims. I shall contend in this monograph that the U.S. court system under the common law has largely failed to honor its responsibilities with respect to the cost-effective resolution of disputes.

The second major function of the courts is the enrichment of the supply of legal rules that private individuals can live, plan and settle by. In many areas, the slowly evolving judicial rule has apparent ad-

1

vantages over legislative rules that tend to be less flexible in form, but more susceptible to sudden change. It is a widely held judgment (Hayek 1983) that the common law upholds the rule of law more effectively than the civil code, and that the courts should consciously take on the function of developing certain bodies of law, albeit on a case-by-case basis. (Eisenberg 1988, 6) I do not deny that the U.S. courts have pursued this second function. Indeed, I shall assert that they have done so with a vengeance, and that in so doing they have largely emasculated the rule of law in this country.

Four foundational principles allegedly govern the manner in which law is established and changed by the courts in a common law system, namely: objectivity, support, replicability and responsiveness. Let me review them each in turn.

In a complex, impersonal and unofficially religious society, like that of the United States, courts derive legitimacy, in substantial part, from their objectivity. Objectivity derives in part from evident impartiality, which requires the courts to be free of ties to the parties, and from universality, which requires the courts to resolve disputes by establishing and applying rules that are applicable not only to the immediate dispute, but to all similarly situated disputes. I shall contend that late twentieth century U.S. courts have failed to maintain such objectivity on a consistent basis.

Even when courts sustain high standards of objectivity, as defined above, the rules that emerge should also be supported by the general standards of the society or by the special standards of the legal system (Eisenberg 1988). For, if the courts resolved disputes by reasoning from other types of standards, there would be no institution to which a member of society could go to vindicate a claim of right based on existing standards. The rooting of common law rules in existing standards provides important support-legitimacy for an institution that is not conceived as representative, and that is deliberately structured in a way that limits its accountability and responsiveness to the citizenry as a whole. In the absence of such support-legitimacy, disputes over past transactions will be resolved by applying rules that have been articulated after the transaction has occurred. I shall contend that the erosion of the role of precedent and of the application of *stare decisis* by the U.S. courts during the second half of the twentieth century has severely eroded, if not entirely destroyed, the support-legitimacy of the common law.

In a complex society, private citizens who desire to resolve disputes or to make plans on the basis of the law normally must consult a lawyer. In the vast majority of instances, the institution that determines the law is not the courts, but the legal profession. In such circumstances, it is important that lawyers should be able to replicate the process of judicial reasoning. The principle of replicability serves as a coordinating device through which the reasoning of the profession can flow (Eisenberg 1988). An important aspect of the principle of replicability is that the courts employ a consistent methodology across cases. I shall contend that the U.S. common law system has failed to preserve such replicability across major and growing areas of the law.

Given that the courts are not structured to be directly responsive to the citizenry as a whole, they should be responsive to, though of course they are not obligated to follow, what the legal profession has to say. The discourse to which courts are obligated to be responsive basically occurs in two areas. The first is in the context of a particular case in which discourse is effected through briefs and oral argument and through lawyers' decisions whether to raise claims or defenses. The second is in the wider context of the profession as a whole, entered after final decision in the particular case is rendered. Discourse in this wider arena takes the form of law reviews, books and monographs, together with other exchanges among members of the bar. I shall contend that responsiveness to the wider arena has significantly deteriorated in the U.S. common law system, not least because of the increasing politicization of the bench and the widening role of the non-specialist jury during the second half of the twentieth century.

Central to the social functions and the foundational principles of the common law system is the concept of doctrinal stability as encapsulated in the institutional principle of *stare decisis*. Under that principle, the *ratio decidendi*, holding, or rule of a precedent is binding upon subsequent cases, within broad limits, if the precedent satisfies certain formal conditions, such as having been rendered by a court of a relevant level in a relevant jurisdiction.

Stare decisis clearly gives effect to the principle of objectivity, requiring the courts to behave impartially and universally in dispensing the law, and discouraging a court from deciding cases on the basis of propositions that it would be unwilling to apply to all similarly situated disputants. It also reinforces the principle that the rules that emerge will reflect the special standards of the legal system, on which legitimacy is derived, and that such rules will be responsive to legitimate legal discourse. Self-evidently, *stare decisis* supports the principle that the law should be replicable throughout the legal profession. For these reasons, *stare decisis* plays a major role in supporting the social function of the courts in the resolution of disputes.

Stare decisis also plays a major role in supporting the social function of the courts in enriching the supply of legal rules. The most salient aspect of this role is the protection of justifiable reliance, without which there can be no rule of law. A tension between *stare decisis* and the evolution of new legal rules in response to changing circumstances inevitably exists. Nevertheless, the standard of doctrinal stability cannot survive any general retreat from the principle of *stare decisis*. It will be my contention in this monograph that the retreat from *stare decisis* in the U.S. common law system is a predictable consequence of the institutional characteristics of the U.S. legal system and that this retreat is now sufficiently extensive as to challenge the validity of the common law system. For what is left now—the surviving kernel of a once robust system of law—is a high-cost, subjective, unresponsive, non-replicable and essentially illegitimate legal system predicated more on the rule of men that on the rule of law.

2. The Ideal of the Common Law

Among the nations of Western Europe, the English alone successfully conveyed the essential elements of their medieval customary legal system into a modern common law system. They did so by overcoming powerful criticism and almost insurmountable obstacles (Hogue 1985, 241). The English common law system survived several periods of political crisis which seriously disturbed the balance between three elements fundamental to the English constitution—the prerogative of the Crown, the privileges of Parliament, and the individual rights to personal security, personal liberty and private property.

The general rules of the common law might well have disappeared in the fifteenth century as a consequence of dynastic disputes known as the *War of the Roses*. The central powers of governmental law enforcement were so eroded by these disputes that the weak could no longer secure justice in the royal courts. Disintegration back into feudalism was avoided only after 1485 when King Henry VII acceded to the throne and established the House of Tudor. The common law again might have succumbed in the sixteenth century when certain English monarchs nurtured Roman law at the expense of medieval customary systems. King Henry VIII favored Roman law but was satisfied instead to manipulate the medieval constitution, especially after the break with Rome and the onset of the English Reformation.

The common law again was threatened throughout much of the seventeenth century by theories of divine right monarchy that greatly influenced the House of Stuart. Government by unrestrained divine right surely would have produced subservient judges sitting in prerogative courts responsive to the monarch's will. The common law escaped such emasculation as a consequence of the Glorious Revolution of 1688 and the flight of King James II.

5

Perhaps its most serious challenge (yet unresolved), however, was the emergence in the eighteenth century of the legislative sovereignty of Parliament which created the possibility of the emasculation of the common law by means of statute. In 1783, William Blackstone, justice of the Court of Common Pleas and Vinerian professor of English law in Oxford University, claimed that the competence of Parliament was so great that he knew "of no power in the ordinary forms of the constitution that is vested with authority to control it" (Blackstone 1973).

In the view of many common law scholars (Hogue 1985, 244), however, the legislative sovereignty of the English Parliament has not destroyed the common law doctrine of *stare decisis* nor has it emasculated the common law doctrine of established legal principles. Its early maturity and technical complexity has provided the common law with formidable protection in the form of a powerful special interest, namely the judge and lawyer lobby. Economic interests, in the form of property owners, also resolutely defended the common law from legislative overthrow, at least until the early twentieth century, when economic interests became more diffuse and the common law defense of property rights became less unambiguous.

The expansion of western European civilization from the late sixteenth century onwards, and most significantly, the widening reach of the British Empire, scattered elements of the English common law across much of the globe. Notably, from the perspective of this monograph, English colonists on the Atlantic seaboard introduced common law to the American continent, while French and Spanish colonists introduced laws originally derived from Roman law. As the British Empire asserted its dominance, the common law traditions predominated, with the exception of Louisiana and also of certain territories acquired from Spain.

The English colonists brought to America the law of England as it stood in the seventeenth and eighteenth centuries. When the colonies broke away from England in the course of the American Revolution, they framed arguments about their rights taken straight from Blackstone's *Commentaries*, the classical statement of the common law: "The enormous popularity of Blackstone in the most formative period of American national institutions may go far to explain why American law kept close to English law" (Hogue 1986, 250)

What then was the *ideal* eighteenth century vision of the common law that eventually evolved out of medieval England and how effectively was this ideal transported to the United States following the War of Revolution? It is important to address these issues before proceeding to critique the *reality* of the common law as it now manifests itself in late twentieth century America.

Foremost among the ideas that constituted the eighteenth century vision is the idea of the *supremacy of law*, a concept also captured by such phrases as the *rule of law* and *due process*. This idea implies that there are limits to the power of ruling, that all government agencies and the law courts themselves must operate according to known rules and procedures. The rule of law is always difficult to apply in the face of ideas of sovereignty, be they from medieval kings or from the modern U.S. Congress, which admits no limitation on the power of ruling. Yet, this idea was at the heart of the ideal version of the common law.

In his influential magnum opus on *The Law of the Constitution* (1987), Albert Venn Dicey cited the supremacy of the law as the chief characteristic of the old law of the English courts: "The law is the highest estate to which the king succeeds, for both he and all his subjects are ruled by it, and without it there would be neither king nor realm." According to Dicey, the supremacy of the law, in turn, was a principle that corresponded to three other concepts, namely: (1) the absence of arbitrary power on the part of the government to punish citizens or to commit acts against life or property; (2) the subjection of every individual, whatever his rank or condition, to the ordinary law of the realm and to the jurisdiction of the ordinary tribunals; and (3) a predominance of the legal spirit in English institutions.

Despite the fact that Americans appeared to derive their individual rights from the general principles laid down in their Constitution and in the first ten amendments, Dicey considered the United States to be a typical instance of a country living under the rule of law, because she had inherited the English traditions. Leoni (1961) strongly endorses Dicey's judgment, noting that a written bill of rights was not considered to be necessary even by the Founding Fathers and that judicial decisions have always been accorded high importance in the political system of the United States in so far as the rights of individuals are concerned.

Hayek (1955) centered attention on four features of the rule of law that coalesce largely with Dicey's description. According to Hayek, the generality, equality and certainty or replicability of the law, as well as the requirement that administrative discretion must always be subject to review by independent courts are: "really the crux of the matter, the decisive point on which it depends whether the Rule of Law prevails or not." (Hayek 1955, 54) This idea implies that there are limits to the power of ruling; that all government agencies, including the law courts themselves, must operate according to known rules and procedures: that adherence to the rule of law may be the only means of preserving the enjoyment of private rights and personal freedoms. (Hogue 1985, 252)

A second idea passed down from the Middle Ages relates to the work of the courts in the legal system and the doctrine of judicial precedent. The dignity of medieval royal courts was impressive. The royal judges, the repositories of the legal tradition, exercised the right to control all matters of procedure; from judging the initial grounds of a legal action to the enforcement of any judgment on that action. When judges failed to maintain the high standards of learning and disinterested action expected of them, the English feudal barons, churchmen and merchants insisted on reform. (Hogue 1985, 253)

In the Middle Ages, common law court decisions were recorded, and occasionally the record would be consulted. For the most part, however, the common law lived more in the memories of judges and practitioners than on plea rolls and reports. The law was largely judge-made, and even when the law was changed by action of the king's council or by Parliament, judges participated in the change. It is an essential feature of the common law system that its principles are derived from decisions in actual cases, in which judges play the predominant role.

A third important element underpinning the common law is the writ system. This is so even though the writ system was abolished by legislation in England during the nineteenth century. English lawyers were content to dispense with those old forms of action because they had become embedded in the common law. The full catalogue of writs, known as the *Register of Writs*, was the framework of the common law.

Let me briefly review the central elements of the common law as they had evolved by the late nineteenth century towards the end of what may be loosely referred to as the *classical period*. These elements best reflect the ideal of the common law that has been advanced in this chapter.

There is no concept more central to the common law than that of property. The legal conception of property is that there are a bundle of rights over resources which the owner is free to exercise and whose exercise is protected from interference by others. Property thus creates "a zone of privacy in which owners can exercise their will over things without being answerable to others" (Cooter and Ulen 1988, 91). As individuals depart from the state of nature, where natural law allows them to defend property from interference, into civil society, where they surrender this right to government, they enter into an agreement which commits government to uphold their natural rights to life, liberty and property (Locke 1690). This agreement is the social contract which includes the fundamental laws of property.

The two normative principles of property law that governed the ideal of the common law were: (1) minimize the harm caused by private disagreements over resource allocation; and (2) minimize the obstacles to private agreements over resource allocation. In pursuit of these principles, the courts developed two alternative responses to situations where illegal interference came from another *private* citizen, namely *legal* or *equitable* remedies.

The principal legal remedy was the payment of compensatory damages by the plaintiff to the defendant. The general rule in common law courts was that legal remedies would be applied unless there was clear evidence that the award of money damages would under-compensate the plaintiff.

Equitable relief, often in the form of an injunction, consisted of an order by the court directing the defendant to perform an act or to refrain from acting in a particular manner.

Economic analysis (Coase 1960) now informs us that legal remedies tend to be efficient when transactions costs are high and that injunctions tend to be efficient when transaction costs are low (the *Coase theorem*). Put differently, owners should be protected against externalities of the private-bads type by the injunctive remedy and against externalities of the public-bads type by compensatory damages. (Cooter and Ulen 1988, 17)

All property owners in a civil society are concerned by the prospect that they may be required to sell their property to the government, without any guarantee that they will be paid their reservation price. The *takings power* thus described is also called the right of *eminent domain* or the right of *condemnation*. The common law in England, where there is no written constitution, deals with the sovereign's right to condemn private property and compel its sale to the Crown by requiring that the taking must be for a public purpose and that the owner must be justly compensated. In the United States, this common law presumption was codified into the Constitution through the fifth amendment. State constitutions generally impose similar constraints.

By the late nineteenth century, the U.S. common law had enunciated the central principles of a *bargain theory of contracts* as the basis for contract law. The approach adopted was that of isolating and abstracting the minimal elements of a typical bargain and of asserting that those elements were necessary for a binding contract in every case. This approach was so widely adopted that it is often referred to as the classical theory of contract.

The classical theory of contract asserted that a promise was legally enforceable if it was given as part of a voluntary bargain and was unenforceable otherwise. In determining whether or not a bargain had been struck, the common law developed three necessary and sufficient conditions, namely the presence of offer, acceptance and consideration. "Offer" and "acceptance" had the same meaning in this context as in ordinary speech. The doctrine of consideration was a technical concept describing what the promisor received in the exchange from the promisee. This element perfected a bargain and made it legally enforceable.

Under classical theory a court would not inquire as to whether the consideration was adequate. Hard bargains, even bargains that a reasonable man would regard as unfair, were enforceable under this doctrine. The court's sole concern would be the presence or absence of consideration, not its adequacy. It was enough for the court that the contracting partners had found the consideration to be adequate at the time the bargain was struck.

The classical theory also had an answer to the question: what should be the remedy for breaking enforceable promises? The answer was that the victim was entitled to *expectation damages*, defined as a payment by the breaching party of a sum of money just sufficient to make the victim as well off as he would have been had the promise been kept. Only rarely would the courts grant the alternative equitable relief of *specific performance,* whereby the parties would be ordered to perform their sides of the bargain. According to classical doctrine, the existence of a bargain established enforceability; and the expected value of a bargain measured damages.

The term *tort* is French, derived from the Latin word *torquere*, to twist, and means a private wrong or injury. (Cooter and Ulen, 1988, 326) Under the ideal of the common law, torts were of limited reach and achieved legal status only where contracts failed to regulate relationships. There was a classical theory that specified the essential elements of a tort, much as did the classical theory in contracts. This theory enjoyed substantial acceptance in America at the end of the nineteenth century.

The purpose of classical theory was to protect the interests of individuals in their property and to protect persons from damage by others. Three elements were distinguished, namely: (1) breach of a duty owed to the plaintiff by the defendant; (2) harm suffered by the plaintiff; and (3) the breach being the immediate or proximate cause of the harm. Although the distinction between intentional and unintentional harm was important, going to the magnitude of the remedy, the focus of tort law itself was not on the mental state of the wrongdoer (or tortfeasor) but rather on the fact that a duty of care had been violated.

The duty of care to which potential tortfeasors were held was the negligence standard of reasonable care which depended on the norms, practices and values of ordinary people. The breach of duty had to give rise to measurable damages, which were prescribed narrowly. Thus, doing something dangerous that caused no harm did not constitute an actionable tort. The courts were willing to compensate for medical costs, but reluctant to compensate for emotional harm, distress or loss of companionship. Until the nineteenth century, a person's action died with him, affording no remedy for a victim's estate.

The third element of a tort concerned the connection between the wrong and the harm; the former must cause the latter. This was strictly required. For the plaintiff to recover, the defendant's breach of duty to the plaintiff must be, not just the cause-in-fact of the plaintiff's injury, but also the *proximate cause*. There had to be a natural and continuous sequence of events which linked the act to the injury, unbroken by any new independent action which produced its own event and injury. Historically common law would not countenance tort suits directed at deep pocket defendants where proximate cause could not be established.

Although criminal law is largely governed by statutes, many of these statutes are codifications of earlier common law. The minimal elements of a crime were defined by the common law courts. Fault is the failure to fulfill an obligation. In every crime there is fault. However, fault was not sufficient to justify criminal prosecution. The intent to harm (or *mens rea*) was necessary to justify criminal prosecution in cases involving personal injury. The first element of a crime, therefore, was intent.

The second element of a crime concerned the physical act(s) which created the harm. In torts, the harm is private, whereas with crimes the harm is public. This explains why tort suits are brought by victims (the plaintiffs) whereas criminal prosecutions are brought by the state.

The elements so far described—criminal intent and public harm—characterize the criminal act. Two further elements characterize the legal consequences. The first is punishment, which can take several forms, ranging from fines in excess of compensation to probation, imprisonment, or execution. The second is the standard of proof required by law. In a civil action, the plaintiff must prove his case by the preponderance of the evidence, or in certain tortious actions clear and convincing evidence. In a criminal action, the state must prove its case beyond a reasonable doubt. Taken together, these four elements constituted the ideal of the common law with respect to crime and punishment.

The ideal of the common law, then, is the development of law by means of judicial precedents, the use of the jury to determine the material facts of a case, and the definition of numerous causes of action. These ideals constitute the principal, valuable legacy of the medieval law to the modern law notwithstanding a number of oddities (e.g. the inability of heirs to sue for compensation in cases where the victim was killed in an accident) that were rectified, if at all, by legislation. Unfortunately, these ideals have been eroded and disfigured by the U.S. judicial system during the second half of the twentieth century, not least because the erosion of the U.S. constitutional republic by the forces of democratic majoritarianism has exposed law and justice to the pressures of the political marketplace.

3. The Common Law in Public Choice Perspective

The U.S. common law system is appropriately analyzed, as part of the more general political market-place, from the perspective of the interest group approach to politics (McCormick & Tollison 1981). In this approach, politicians are modeled as providing a brokering function in the political market for wealth transfers. Voters, confronted with individual incentives to abstain from voting or at least to remain rationally ignorant of political activity, tend not to be decisive in the wealth transfer market (Tullock 1993). Relatively small, homogeneous special interest groups, capable of effective political organization, "demand" wealth transfers. Other more general, heterogeneous groups, incapable of effective political organization, "supply" such transfers. Politicians effect political market equilibrium, balancing benefits against costs at the margin, in return for some balance of expected wealth and expected votes. The public bureaucracy, which includes the court system, enforces the deals that are struck in the political market-place.

The concepts of "demand" and "supply" in this stylized model require a somewhat special interpretation. (Rowley, Shughart & Tollison 1987). "Demand" consists of the willingness to pay, in the form either of money transfers or of votes, by well-organized special interests, in return for wealth transfers carrying a positive net present value. Such positive expected returns, which represent rent and not profit, induce rent-seeking behavior (Tullock 1967, 1993). "Supply" consists of the unwillingness or inability of those from whom wealth transfers are sought, at the margin, to protect themselves by making countervailing offers of money transfers or votes to the balancing mechanism. Evidently, there are connotations of coercion associated with this concept of "supply."

14

Many of the public institutions of the U.S. legal system were developed to facilitate the monarchy's efforts to centralize and consolidate their power (Benson 1990, 87). These institutions now operate in a representative democracy. Yet, because the legal system is intimately bound up in the legitimate use of coercive force in society, it must be viewed as an integral part of the political process. Special interest groups have strong incentives to try to influence the behavior of the legal system. All areas of law are subject to interest group manipulation through the legislative process. Moreover, once laws are passed, the administration of justice is also influenced by interest groups. Attempts are made to influence the courts, the police, the juries, the prosecutors, the witnesses and the rest of the legal system to assure that laws favorable to special interest groups are enforced.

4.   All the World's a Stage

The United States legal system is based on adversary proceedings which are unique to the Anglo-Saxon tradition. It provides a stage on which many players perform, each responding to specific incentives and constraints in a rational expected utility-maximizing way. In this chapter, I subject the behavior of each of the principal players to public choice analysis, setting the scene for a review of the common law play itself in *Chapter 5.*

(A) The Courts

Courts in the United States are publicly-owned facilities provided to the general public at zero or near zero prices. Courts that are composed of long-term appointee judges (all the federal courts and approximately half the state courts) are fully-fledged bureaucracies. Courts that are composed of shorter-term, elected judges confront incentives and constraints that render them directly vulnerable to electoral pressures. In the latter courts, the lower the level of the judge and the shorter his term of office, the more intense his political involvement predictably will be.

Courts are like any form of public property. When ownership rights are not clearly assigned, and when prices are not charged to ration its use, the resource is over-used and inefficiently allocated. Ostensibly available on a first-come, first-served basis, the tragedy of the commons results, ameliorated only by an implicit pricing system that favors wealthy individuals and well-heeled organizations who gain privileged access to the justice system. Those who administer the court system typically do not comprehend the nature of the problem. Chief Justice Burger, for example, complained that the courts were over-crowded and that there was an excess demand for courts' services. (Benson 1990, 99) In fact, the existence of a queue simply indicates that the service is under-priced.

The over-crowding of the courts implies that rationing must occur, a process which favors those who can most afford to stand in line. Since places in line cannot be auctioned off or traded, at least overtly, all litigants pay essentially the same price for use, a price that bears no necessary relationship to the importance of the case. The rationing process can be manipulated, especially in civil court cases where customers come in competing pairs. Delay is often an attractive product to a better-heeled customer allowing him an opportunity to wear down a less well-heeled opponent. Given that courts do not efficiently price their services, an incentive is provided for customers to outspend their opponents, driving the latter into disadvantageous settlements by the threat of ever-escalating legal costs. In criminal cases, the court system encourages foot-dragging by criminals and unwarranted prosecution by prosecutors and the police.

Excess demands on the civil court system often spill over and downgrade the criminal system and vice-versa because civil and criminal lawsuits compete for essentially the same resources. Thus the waste and inefficiency associated with common access also distorts justice across the common law system. In this sense, the public production of the common law imposes negative externalities upon society at large.

The tragedy of the commons manifest in the U.S. court system could be avoided by the introduction of market-clearing prices. Such a price mechanism would discourage frivolous, low-valued use of the justice system, just as it would deny access to those who could not pay. Predictably, a number of special interests would resist such a solution. The legal profession, through its mouthpieces, the American Bar Association and the Association of Trial Lawyers of America, would lobby powerfully against any measure that reduced the volume of litigation. City and state governments would also lobby to avoid the bankruptcy that might ensue if civil cases against abuses were to be concluded successfully against them in a timely fashion. Insurance companies clearly have a major stake in slow-moving litigation as do tenant associations defying the eviction of members for non-payment of rent. (Benson 1990, 118). Many special interests actively seek (and seek successfully) mediocre, or even downright incompetent court performance.

(B) The Judges

It is widely believed that U.S. judges (federal judges most especially) enjoy considerable independence from the interest group pressures that dominate the market-place of politics. The independence is derived both from the rules that govern judicial tenure and from the rules of judicial procedure. It is supposedly fortified by the oaths of loyalty to the Constitution that all judges—state as well as federal—are required to swear prior to assuming office.

Article III of the United States Constitution provides for the appointment, rather than for the election, of federal judges, guarantees that such judges have life tenure in office and provides that Congress may not reduce their salaries while they remain in office. In a number of states similar provisions exist, although protection is not as extensive as that offered to the federal judges. These constitutional guarantees certainly protect federal (and some state) judges from flagrant political pressure, though a guaranteed nominal salary offers only limited financial security in an inflationary economy. They do not provide an absolute barrier against political pressure.

First, each federal judge is appointed to office only following nomination by the President and confirmation by the Senate—a uniquely political route to judicial office. In the case where the Presidency and the Senate is under single party control, the path is open for appointments that reflect a common ideology and that are susceptible to a particular group of special interests. Where power is divided, only extremely compliant, flexible and non-assertive individuals will make their way to office. Such personalities will respond equally flexibly to the prevailing winds that blow across Capitol Hill throughout their terms in office.

Special interest groups have obvious incentives to influence the recruitment of judges. Eisenstein (1988) found that bureaucrats, lawyers, bar associations and various other organized interest groups actively seek to influence judicial appointments at all levels of government. The special interest circus occasionally reaches farcical levels in Supreme Court appointments, notably, in recent years, in the successful attempt to derail the nomination of Robert Bork and in the ultimately unsuccessful, but vicious attempt to derail the nomination of Clarence Thomas. Many judgeships in the United States are political rewards for individuals who have demonstrated past support for powerful interest groups. Such individuals often have little understanding of the law itself and little or no respect for precedent and *stare decisis*. Usually, the latter qualities are not attractive to the special interests.

Second, even though individual judges cannot be removed from office once appointed, the integrity of the judicial system itself may be threatened if judges attempt to uphold the Constitution against the combined authority of Congress and the President. This indeed was the case in 1937 when Justice Roberts of the U.S. Supreme Court dishonored his oath of office and switched position in *West Coast Hotel Co. v. Parrish* to uphold a state minimum-wage statute. (Rowley 1992, 111). This "switch in time that saved nine" avoided an all-out attempt to pack the Supreme Court with New Deal protagonists by increasing the number of justices from nine to fifteen. Such a threat need be leveled only rarely to bring the judicial system to heel for several decades and to impose an attitude of judicial deference that is inimical to the concept of separation of powers.

Third, even though the salaries of federal judges cannot be lowered by Congress, their offices are entirely dependent on the flow of annual appropriations from Congress. If the judiciary were to stand resolutely against unconstitutional behavior by Congress (as it attempted to do throughout the early 1930's) budgets might be sharply reduced to the discomfiture of individual judges. If the judiciary resisted the unlawful behavior of the executive branch, it is not inconceivable that the executive branch would refuse to enforce its judgments. Threats of this kind, however implicit, may sharply influence the judicial behavior of judges and justices who were not appointed in the first place because of their jurisprudential brilliance or the firmness of their independent resolve.

Fourth, although the salaries of the judges cannot be lowered, they need not be increased to keep pace with inflation and rising living standards. In consequence, the annual salaries of all federal judges are substantially lower in real terms than they were in 1900 and about one-third lower than they were in 1940, (Posner 1985, 32), despite massive increases in per capita U.S. income over these time periods. Current salaries are unattractive to high-flying lawyers in private practice, further downgrading intellectual quality and personal vigor at all levels of the federal judiciary, notwithstanding the prestige attached to appellate court judgeships and (especially) to positions on the Supreme Court.

All judges are required to take an oath "to support the Constitution" and all federal judges another oath to decide cases "agreeably to the Constitution." So the lawful judge is constrained by the Constitution. Where the Constitution is unambiguous, the lawful judge, in principle, has no option but to uphold its meaning, even though he may disagree with that meaning, and even though majority opinion may be hostile to that meaning. If a judge or justice cannot accept the burdens of this constraint, he has two options, namely either to refuse or to relinquish office or to become unlawful and betray the oath of office. Few have taken the former route. Many have taken the unlawful route and have abandoned the text of the Constitution, whether in pursuit of private political agendas or in deference to special interest pressures (Rowley 1992, 97).

As Posner (1985, 17) makes clear: "in a system in which judges are appointed by politicians, it would be unrealistic to expect all or most judges to be apolitical technicians." It is not surprising, therefore, to find that the most influential U.S. judges—John Marshall (who received only six weeks training in law), Oliver Wendell Holmes, Louis Brandeis, Benjamin Cardozo, William Howard Taft, Felix Frankfurter, Robert Jackson, Hugo Black, Earl Warren, William Brennan, William Rehnquist and Learned Hand—were all politically motivated rather than jurisprudentially learned. Few of those would have made their way to high judicial ranking under peer review of the kind practiced in England and Wales.

Posner (1990 and 1995) challenges the normative validity of the "faithful agent" notion of the good judge, evidencing doubts as to whether there is any moral duty to obey the law (Posner 1990, 137). He makes it clear that judges, even Supreme Court justices, will not be bound by rules, at least not completely, and that they will impose their own preferences in the shaping of the law. Judicial independence, which in England guarantees the insulation of judges from politics, in America fosters the exercise of political power by individual judges. "Judicial independence has not taken our judges out of politics; in our political culture, it has put the judges securely in politics." (Posner 1985, 19).

If the so-called *judicial titans,* who are revered or hated for creating U.S. law, are essentially creatures of politics, what is the predictable motivation of the ordinary appellate judge with secure tenure (be it a federal court of appeals judge or a Supreme Court Justice)? This question has been answered empirically (Higgins and Rubin 1980; Kimenyi, Shughart and Tollison 1985) and theoretically (Posner 1993), with fairly consistent results.

Higgins and Rubin (1980) developed and tested a theory based on the assumption that judges maximized some combination of personal wealth and ideology subject to constraints imposed by judgment reversals, politics and seniority. In this theory, judges are assumed to benefit from imposing their values upon society through precedent-setting opinions. They also benefit from increased wealth, which is enhanced by an absence of judgment reversals by superior courts and by promotion within the judicial system. Empirical tests decisively rejected this theory. Judicial discretion appears to be unconstrained, with age and seniority insignificant, precedent unimportant and no evidence of effective policing through appellate review.

Kimenyi, Shughart and Tollison (1985) focused more narrowly on personal economic reward as the factor that motivates judges. They determined empirically that judicial output is influenced by economic factors. They concluded that the presence or absence of incentives to economic efficiency are as relevant to the judiciary as they are to other areas of human behavior.

In a far-reaching theoretical study, Posner (1993) outlined a positive economic theory of judicial voting. Essentially, he argued that rational judges pursue instrumental and consumption goals of the same general kind and in the same general way as private individuals. The vast majority of judges are not Six Six, intent on changing the world, or saints, devoid of human weaknesses, biases and foibles. They are not, for the most part, either power seekers, like some politicians, or truth seekers, like many scientists.

The judiciary operates on a non-profit basis and so judges, on average, do not work as hard as lawyers of comparable age and experience. The enormous caseload increases in recent decades have been accommodated mainly by expansions in staff, who are eligible for quality increases and bonuses. Federal judges of the same rank are all paid the same, regardless of stature and productivity. Leisure predictably has a lower opportunity cost than is the case in private practice. Those who do work hard are motivated by the desire for popularity (with the bar rather than with litigants) and by the desire for prestige among their peers.

Judges do not like to be reversed but this aversion, according to Posner, does not figure largely in the judicial utility function. It is nonexistent in the case of Supreme Court Justices, and fairly unimportant in the case of court of appeals judges. Reversal rates do not appear to affect district judges' chances of promotion. Judges do like to vote, however, not least because this is the symbol of their power, and to be published, which is their best prospect of immortality. By voting with the majority—what Posner calls "going along voting,"—a judge can maximize the pursuit of leisure without noticeably sacrificing the deference that his voting power attracts from the bar.

Posner's theory helps to explain why judges adhere to stare decisis, but not rigidly. Rigid adherence would eliminate discretion and would reduce the perceived power of office. "Going-along voting" and "live-and-let-live opinion-joining" are leisure-seeking activities, even though they are not far distant from judicial log-rolling, which would attract public hostility.

However, Posner's theory ultimately does not allay suspicion that judges who cannot be removed from office and whose salaries cannot be cut retain considerable discretion to pursue personal agendas in their judicial decision-making. There is no obvious reason why judges should be enamored of economic efficiency for its own sake. Law and economics scholars, therefore, have been forced to fall back on dubious arguments concerning the nature of the litigation process itself (*Chapter 5*) to justify their assertion that the common law is economically efficient.

(C) The Lawyers

Lawyers did not always play a significant role in the evolution of the common law. Prior to the thirteenth century, indeed, legal advisors, professional councilors and pleaders were not allowed by custom. Individuals not skilled in the art of pleading were seen to be less likely to be able to conceal their guilt. Moreover, one litigant might be unable to hire a skilled spokesman, while another could, providing the one with an unfair advantage over the other. Ancient principles thus retarded the emergence of the legal profession (Benson 1990, 57).

The earliest records of a pleader identify John de Planez as pleading on behalf of King Henry II. King Richard I employed a permanent contingent of pleaders. As with other common law developments in England, the legal profession was established to provide an additional advantage to the king. The king not only gained an advantage in his own suits; but was able to sell the same privilege to others. King Edward I had a large number of servants or sergeants at law under retainer and a large number of appointees who were their pupils. By 1292, these legal practitioners had acquired some exclusive right to audience. In that year, Edward ordered his justices to provide for a sufficient number of attorneys and apprentices in each county so that the king and the powerful might be well served (Benson 1990, 58).

London had already begun to license two groups of legal professionals—attorneys and pleaders—in 1280. However, the king's justices assumed control of the licensing function in 1292 and severely restricted entry in order to secure monopoly power for those appointed. The legal profession began to take shape. Attorneys and counters became licensed court appointees and formed into a professional group. Those who wished to learn the profession joined the guilds or fraternities that eventually would develop into the Inns of Court, the English law schools. Legal procedures became much more complex and litigation more prolonged. Lawyers, rather than ecclesiastical clerics, became the primary candidates for royal judgeships. Lawyers slowly but inexorably began to tighten their stranglehold over the common law (Benson 1990, 58).

Lawyers have practiced in America since early colonial times with early settlers enjoying a period of free entry into the legal profession. Dispute resolution services were made available by a wide range of *scriveners* drawn from such diverse occupations as the clergy and the taverns (Brough and Kimenyi 1987). This informal bar provided little by way of special training in the law, emphasizing instead skills in penmanship and in dispute resolution. As the colonies became more established and populated with new immigrants trained in English law, pressure mounted for regulation, based on claims that the law had been overrun by *untrained pettifoggers* who posed a nuisance to society. In essence, the main goal of the colonial bar was to restrict access into the profession through a licensed barrier to entry (Rowley 1992, 272).

In its bid to establish exclusivity for the legal profession, the colonial bar established three tiers of regulation. The first, the establishment of training standards and educational requirements for all individuals seeking to practice law, is still an important entry barrier, with accreditation procedures allowing the bar associations not only to restrict entry but also to police the curricula of accredited law schools.

The second tier of regulation, the bar examination, is designed to restrict the number of attorneys permitted to appear before the courts. Maurizi (1974) estimated that, between 1940 and 1950, a ten per cent increase in excess supply of lawyers generated a decrease in bar examination pass rates ranging from one to ten per cent. Royack (1976) determined, in the case of ten out of twelve licensing systems under review, that bar examination failure rates increased systematically over a fifty-eight year period in response to increases in the general unemployment rate. Brough and Kimenyi (1987) found a positive, statistically significant relationship between pass rates in the bar examinations and prior increases in attorney incomes. They also detected an inverse statistical relationship between excess demand for entry and pass rates in the bar examination. Such results are consistent with the hypothesis that the bar examination is used as an entry barrier and not exclusively as a protector of legal standards.

The third tier of regulation, licensure, established the bar as the exclusive enforcer of standards and as the exclusive authority over the number of lawyers who can practice. This is characteristic of the present U.S. legal system. All state bars police the profession through the use of unauthorized practice of law statutes, which make it illegal for unlicensed individuals to practice law. All states have legislated to impose mandatory bar examinations, one section of which is uniform nationwide and the other section of which is written by the state bar association. These examinations are graded by licensed members of the legal profession who are exempt from antitrust regulations following the favorable ruling of the U.S. Supreme Court in *Hoover v. Ronwin* (1984).

Despite the enforcement of entry barriers, the United States has far more lawyers per capita than any other country, 700,000 or seventy per cent of the world's entire supply. Recent studies suggest that, after correcting for other factors, a nation's economic growth is positively correlated with the number of engineers and negatively correlated with the number of lawyers. (Posner 1992, 589). Where there are too many lawyers in a country, incentives exist for them to press for inefficient laws in order to manufacture fee income. The fault lies not only with the legal profession itself, however, but with the growing taste in America for wealth redistributionist litigation. Many Americans have become the world's leading socialists, paying lip-service to capitalism while pursuing the socialization of all risk through the legal process.

There are two different types of lawyer in the United States. The trial lawyer has evolved into an expert at debating the law and swaying the jury (and/or the judge). Court proceedings tend to be dominated by debates over points of law between opposing attorneys (often with the jury excluded) (Tullock 1995c, 11). Some attorneys specialize in manipulating the ordinary people who comprise the jury (Tullock 1990, 16). In some cases, attorneys seek to persuade the jury to bring in verdicts that are contrary to the law, to fall back on what are called the *fireside equities,* for example, to nullify a clear criminal conviction. Judges sometimes make efforts to discipline such breaches of legal ethics. Unfortunately, many judges are tarred with the same feathers as the lawyers, and favor the fireside equities over the established law.

The Anglo-Saxon system allows the parties (or more correctly the attorneys) basic control over the proceedings, with the judge acting as arbiter or referee. Courtroom strategy is extremely important in the adversarial system, which is governed by a complex system of procedural rules. For example, skillful attorneys use procedural objections primarily to interrupt the judge's and jury's train of thought in order to diminish the effectiveness of witness testimony (Tullock 1980, 152). In such circumstances, the relative ability of the lawyers hired by the two parties becomes extremely important in determining the outcome of a case. The adversary system places little or no value on searching for the truth. It is a combat system in which winning is the sole objective. Indeed, the smaller the role played by trial lawyers, the more likely it is that the outcome will be in accordance with the facts (Tullock 1971, 92).

There is a significant element of rent-seeking in the adversarial legal system. Trial lawyers can be viewed from the same perspective as special interest lobbyists. In both cases, government is involved as a vehicle of wealth redistribution. The basic difference between the two is that legal proceedings are subject to more stringent procedural rules. Such rules may serve to increase rather than to ameliorate the social waste from rent-seeking and rent-protection. As with much lobbying of Congress, litigation offers some prospect of a genuine social product. However, the social product itself tends to be lost in a sea of social waste (Tullock 1995a, 17).

The second kind of lawyer does not engage in litigation, but rather specializes in interpreting the current law and in advising clients, for example, on drafting contracts or skirting the edges of the criminal law. This is a large scale enterprise which accounts for the major part of legal work in the United States. Unlike the trial lawyer, who benefits from ambiguities in the law in order to manipulate juries, the writing specialists usually prefer long and detailed codifications that they must master in order to service their clients at high billing rates. Even in this aspect of the law, however, competing attorneys vie in interpreting contracts to exploit unanticipated loopholes (Tullock, 1995b, 17).

Do we want our resources to be put to competitive rent-seeking? There is a real possibility that the rent-seeking costs of a transaction may exceed the social product (Tullock 1996, 17). The cost of employing attorneys to enforce a contract may increase the accuracy of the outcome by an amount valued at less than the attorneys' costs (in aggregate). In such circumstances, eliminating attorneys entirely would boost the nation's wealth, since the work of one attorney to some extent simply cancels out the value of the other (Tullock 1995a, 16).

(D) The Jury

The purpose of a jury system—whatever its form, at whatever point in time—has been either to buttress or to buffer official power. The buttressing jury simply confirmed the view of the holder of power. The buffering jury evolved when accusations needed to be proved to a collection of people and the jury came to represent the wisdom of that community. When that wisdom opposed the ruling power, the jury became a political institution. When it acquired the freedom to disagree with the ruling power without retribution, the jury became a political force (DiPerma 1984, 21).

Most historians place the origin of the Western jury system in classical Athens. The Greek jury, called a dicastery, little resembled a modern jury. The jurors, or dicasts, had to be male, over thirty years of age, full and free citizens, and free of debt. Normally five hundred and one dicasts would serve in a public, or criminal case and two hundred and one in a private, or civil case. Verdict was by majority vote and the ballots—black and white stones—were placed in urns for secrecy. Jurors' names were drawn by lot by the magistrates. Fee-paying, introduced by Pericles in the fifth century, encouraged the poor and elderly to make up the majority of the dicasts, serving essentially as professional jurors. Jurors might be chosen, or volunteer for a specific case precisely because they had knowledge of it. The dicasts were free to ask questions of parties to a case and were provided with all available evidence. The dicasts decided both fact and law and often passed sentence too (DiPerma 1984 25).

The modern jury system, however, is of Anglo-Saxon origin, based on the English jury system introduced when the Normans invaded England in 1066 A.D. There were several precursors to English trial by jury. In the ninth century King Alfred divided the country into tithings, each composed of ten neighboring households. When a dispute occurred, every member of the tithing would debate it. Trial by oath required that a defendant should retell his case repeatedly. Any wavering from the original version would forfeit the case. Compurgation was another mode of trial in which the defendant had to find eleven persons who would swear to his side of the dispute, adding his own vote to make twelve.

At the time of the Norman conquest, trial by ordeal was the most common form of judgment. A defendant would be subjected to such rituals as walking barefoot on hot iron plowshares or reaching into a pot of boiling water. If his skin remained unblemished or uninjured, he would be declared innocent. During most of these rituals, priests and other clergy were present. In the early thirteenth century, Pope Innocent III forbade churchmen to participate. Thereafter, trial by ordeal increasingly gave way to trial by jury.

Throughout the twelfth century, the jury system was restricted mostly to civil matters, primarily property disputes. King Henry II, who reigned from 1154 to 1189, established the Grand Assize, a court of four knights and twelve neighbors, who ruled on challenged claims to land. Juries that found against the king could be charged with attaint, and, if their judgment was reversed by a second jury, attainted jurors could lose their property and/or be imprisoned.

In 1215, the English nobility challenged the supremacy of the king and forced King John to sign the *Magna Carta*. The contemporary idea of the right to jury trial derives from this document. Article 36 of the Magna Carta guarantees the right of inquisition or trial. Article 39 sets out that: "no free man shall be taken or imprisoned...nor shall we send upon him unless by the lawful judgment of his peers, or by the law of the land". These newly guaranteed rights brought jury trials into prominence in England. The right to a trial by jury was supposed to make tyranny impossible, imposing a buffer between the king's will and application of the law (Tullock 1971, 85).

Colonization of British America brought the English jury system to the New World. Trial by jury was guaranteed in some form by the incorporating charters of each colony. Though unanimity among jurors in criminal case verdicts had become English rule, some colonies had provisions for majority rule decisions. The First Continental Congress in 1774 asserted that the colonists had the right to be tried by their peers. The Declaration of Independence declared among its grievances against King George III that he had been depriving colonists "in many cases" of the right of jury trial.

Following victory in the War of Revolution, the sixth amendment to the United States Constitution specifically guaranteed the right to jury trial in all federal criminal cases punishable by more than six months imprisonment. The seventh amendment provided for this right in civil trials. In 1968, a Supreme Court decision, *Duncan v. Louisiana*, held that the sixth amendment had been incorporated into the fourteenth amendment and, therefore, applied to the individual states. At the time the Constitution was written one separate branch of law, equity, functioned without juries. Its descendants still do so today.

The fifth amendment to the Constitution provides that no person shall be held to answer for a capital, or otherwise infamous crime, unless on a presentment or indictment of a Grand Jury. Grand Juries are used to investigate crimes committed within a court's jurisdiction. Persons are indicted if there is sufficient evidence to warrant holding them for trial. The Grand Jury has the right to subpoena witnesses, to question them privately without the presence of their lawyer, and to conduct any investigation that it chooses. As a normal rule, the Grand Jury performs its duties quickly and tends to follow the direction of the prosecuting attorney (Tullock 1990, 14).

Until 1835 the American jury retained its colonial right to decide the law as well as the facts of a case, always assuming the law decided was constitutional. From 1835, the jury lost that right, although defense attorneys frequently attempt to persuade juries to behave unlawfully through nullification of the law. They are successful in such subversive attempts more frequently than most legal scholars choose to acknowledge. In large part, the problem arises because of the low average intelligence and dysfunctional nature of many juries, especially those drawn from inner city populations.

The right to trial by jury in criminal cases is guaranteed constitutionally both at the federal and at the state level, with exceptions for trials in juvenile court and for petty offenses. The Supreme Court has ruled that defendants may waive their right to a jury trial and that plea bargains are not an unconstitutional violation of the defendant's right to trial by jury. The Federal Criminal Code states that a defendant may waive a jury trial only with the approval of the court and the consent of the government. In many state courts, the consent of the prosecutor is not required for a waiver of jury trial rights by the defendant.

Jury verdicts are all but sacrosanct (DiPerma 1984, 19). In criminal cases, only convictions can be appealed to a higher court and only then on points of law—often alleged errors in the judge's charge to the jury. The jury's verdict itself is never the basis for an appeal. Civil cases, however, are somewhat different. The right to trial by jury in civil cases is guaranteed by the sixth amendment. Both parties in a civil suit must agree if the jury right is to be waived. However, the judge may set aside a civil verdict on appeal on the basis either of points of law or of a review of the evidence. The judge may also change the amount of monetary damages awarded by the jury.

Twelve member juries are still common in the United States, especially in criminal cases. In 1970, the Supreme Court ruled in *Williams v. Florida*, that the number twelve had been an: "historical accident, unrelated to the great purposes which gave rise to the jury in the first place." Currently, seven states permit juries of fewer than twelve for misdemeanors. In civil cases, twenty-two states permit juries of fewer than twelve. Six member juries are the minimum number allowed.

There is inconsistency in the law concerning whether verdicts must be unanimous. The U.S. Supreme Court has ruled that the Constitution does not require unanimous verdicts in criminal proceedings. In practice, all federal verdicts, criminal and civil, must be unanimous. A number of states have moved to less than unanimity verdicts at least for some crimes. In civil cases, thirty-one states permit non-unanimous verdicts, and some require only a simple majority. There is a growing interest, nationwide, (trial lawyers excepted) in favor of moving away from unanimity in criminal trials as a means of lowering the incidence of hung juries.

The jury selection process is a controversial aspect of the jury system. There is a large and growing gap between theory and practice in jury selection. In theory, jury selection is supposed to be a random procedure drawing names from some relevant population. That is what is now implied by "a jury of one's peers." Practice is far different. The first stage in jury selection, both for criminal and civil trials, is the *venire*. The *venire* lists eligible jurors drawn from the population of the United States, age eighteen or older, who can communicate in English ("communicate" is broadly interpreted). Most common is the use of voter registration lists.

Since only sixty per cent of eligible voters register, a large part of the population, often minorities, are excluded from this list. A number of jurisdictions attempt to improve the reach of a jury list, not necessarily in any scientific manner. In *Glasser v. United States,* the Supreme Court ruled that jury selection procedures, even though intended to secure competent jurors, had to comport with the concept of the jury as a cross-section of the community. From this judgment the law evolved so that under-representation of "cognizable classes" is now ground for reversal of a verdict if it can be proved that those who prepared the list had the opportunity to discriminate as well as the intent. Racial and ethnic groups and women are held to be unquestionably "cognizable." Others such as the young, poor, religious, and under-educated are argued to be such. Inevitably, run-down inner-city communities, pressured to build juries that reflect the diversity of their populations, end up with juries that are too inept and dysfunctional to dispense justice.

Once the list has been called and the summons sent out, intelligent potential jurors with a significant opportunity cost of time find excuses, including perceived bias, to be excused from duty. Some sixty per-cent of summonsed jurors are successful in avoiding service in this way. Others are rejected by counsel either for cause or by peremptory strikes. Counsel are increasingly advised by experts on the psychological profiles of potential jurors and strike to win, not to ensure justice. The *voir dire* process through which potential jurors are investigated with varying intensity is costly in time and devastating for any notion of "a jury of one's peers." Jury lists are routinely manipulated by counsel. Any unevenness in the quality of opposing counsel thus tilts the jury selection in favor of one party or the other.

Juries typically consist, therefore, of individuals of below average intelligence, of below average income and of below average productivity. They are made up disproportionately of the old, the lame and the unemployed. They are selected to reflect racial and ethnic diversity and implicitly encouraged, therefore, to think of their role in such terms. Lost completely in this potpourri is the notion of a jury trial as a "trial per pais" or, in the famous words of Lysander Spooner (1852), as a "trial by the country—that is by the people." The people who serve on juries, most especially those who serve on high-profile, sequestered juries, tend to be extremely non-random, unusual representatives of the population at large.

If the average jury is made up of individuals of below average intelligence, below average income and below average productivity, the jury system has additionally evolved to ensure that it operates with low levels of information. Potential jurors with above average information concerning the matter in hand tend to be stricken from the panel. Potential jurors who are well-versed in the law find it easy to have themselves removed from consideration. Jurors are so deprived of real information in the court room, because of arcane rules of evidence, (see *Chapter 5*) that many of them literally (maybe even productively) sleep their way through the trial. Juries convict or acquit at whim because jurymen are out of their depth, especially in complex financial trials (Tullock 1988).

This goes to an important issue in the debate over jury trials. Those who strongly favor jury trials frequently argue that the United States is a government of law and not of men. They are grievously mistaken in this perception. Jurors who do not understand the law often overturn it unconsciously. Those who do understand the law and choose to nullify it do so with malice. Those who understand the law but are not presented with the undiluted facts grope blindly for a judgment based on the rhetoric of opposing counsel. To argue for the continued use of the jury suggests a dislike of the current legal code and a desire to have it overturned at will and/or by chance. This is the rule of men and not of law. It may even disintegrate into rule by a very costly and time-consuming lottery.

(E) The Witnesses

In medieval times, witnesses to a crime often acted as jurors to the case, enhancing the relevant information that could be accessed to bring in a true verdict. In late twentieth century America, genuine witnesses are excluded from jury service and are so hobbled by rules of evidence (see *Chapter 5*) that they become pawns moved by rhetoric of counsel. In their place, so-called "expert witnesses" mostly professional liars who repeat under oath whatever counsel has trained them to say, seek to mislead the judge and jury on matters of financial or technical complexity.

The entire problem of dishonest testimony and its prevention bristles with difficulties (Tullock 1971, 97). The basic problem is that it is extremely difficult to detect whether people are lying. Even if there was developed some perfect method of detecting lies, there would still be many reasons why decisions might be incorrect. The human memory is fallible; most people are poor observers; and judges make their own errors. Nevertheless, eliminating lying testimony would be a major advance.

The principal method of detecting lies used in American courtrooms involves a combination of examination and cross-examination by counsel and looking intently at the witness's face in the hope that his expression will indicate that he is lying. This method is not very good. Contrary objective evidence or conflicting testimony is another method, although that also may be suspect. Even if a witness is discredited on one point, that may not mean that the remainder of his evidence is also tainted. The average individual is not a good observer, a fact that has been proven by innumerable experiments, and may well be mistaken on part of his evidence simply because he observed badly.

Better ways of telling whether witnesses are lying are currently available, though they are much under-utilized (Tullock 1971, 100). Falling under the general heading of "lie-detectors," they are the subject of heated debate, despite evident technical advantages. Lie detectors measure a witness's blood pressure, evaluate the electrical conductivity of his skin as well as several other phenomena that are not visible to the naked eye. They are not foolproof or error proof. But to a much less degree is the naked eye. A sensible procedure would be to take all the evidence, including the lie detector test into account simultaneously, allowing the judge, the jury and opposing counsel to see the dials as well as the witness's face.

In a court system where the loser does not pay the winner's costs, there is a constant temptation to call too many witnesses, to strengthen one's case and to confuse the jury. This is another weakness of the adversary common law system that I shall address in *Chapter 5*.

5. The Play's the Thing

In the view of Posner (1979), three factors lead to wealth maximizing efficiency in the common law: (1) wealth maximization is closely related to utilitarianism, and the formative period of the common law as we know it today, roughly 1800–1950, was a period when utilitarianism was the dominant political ideology in England and America; (2) judges lack effective tools for enriching an interest group or social class other than by increasing society's wealth as a whole in which the favored group presumably will share; and (3) the process of common law adjudication leads to the survival of efficient rules.

I take issue categorically with Posner's (1979) viewpoint. It is true that the early twentieth century common law (classical law) contained many efficiency-enhancing factors. As I shall demonstrate in *Chapter 6*, however, the benign nineteenth century influence of utilitarian philosophy has been swept away dramatically during the twentieth century under the influence of socialist ideology combined with pervasive legal rent-seeking (Tullock 1996). The consequence is a late twentieth century common law that is scarcely recognizable as a descendant of its classical predecessor. Judges indeed have found it possible to change legal rules so as to benefit favored special interest groups, most notably the Association of Trial Lawyers of America, and they have done so with a vengeance. Where the judges have not moved, federal and state legislators, dominated by lawyers, have enacted statutes to ensure that legal rent-seeking is profitable for an ever-growing cohort of American attorneys.

Let me focus briefly on point (3) in Posner's argument which offers a more subtle, if equally unfounded, process-oriented justification for common law efficiency (Rubin 1977). It is argued that the courts will be utilized more frequently to resolve disputes when the

existing rules relevant to that dispute are inefficient and less frequently when the rules are efficient. Once efficient rules have
evolved, their existence lowers the incentive for future litigation,
thus raising the probability that such rules will endure.

In this perspective, efficiency is the outcome of evolution generated by the myopic utility-maximizing decisions of potential litigants rather than by any efficiency predilections of judges. Rubin
applies this theory to accident liability law and demonstrates that
where both parties to a dispute have an ongoing interest in efficient
outcomes (e.g. insurance companies), efficient evolution is a predictable consequence of litigation. His result is not general. If only
one party to a dispute is far-sighted, precedent will evolve in favor
of that party, as occurred, for example, in nineteenth century nuisance law, which tended to favor large corporations. If there is no
far-sightedness, the status quo may persist despite the imposition of
significant efficiency losses on both parties to the dispute. High litigation costs, imposed by legal rent-seeking, may also impede litigation on inefficient rules and obstruct the efficient outcome.

Cooter and Kornhauser (1980) abandon the suspect assumptions
of Rubin and model legal evolution as a Markov process. They determine that blind evolution will not take the legal system to an efficient equilibrium. Instead, the common law settles down to a sta-
ble state in which each legal rule prevails for a fixed amount of
time. The system never settles down to a situation in which the best
rule prevails forever, even when bad rules are litigated more frequently than good rules and even when judges are more likely to
replace bad rules by good rules than vice versa. In an environment
where precedent and *stare decisis* has been all but jettisoned, as is
the case in the United States, this interpretation has the commend-
able advantage (at least to the non-specialist) of corresponding with
common sense (Rowley 1989, 377).

It is not possible in this short monograph to review in detail the
institutional deficiencies that lead to continuing inefficiencies in the
entire common law process. Let me instead focus attention on the
nature of such deficiencies in one important branch, namely the
criminal law. I shall attempt to draw together the implications for
criminal law efficiency of what we now know (from *Chapter 4*)

about the principal actors playing out their individual roles under the arcane rules that dominate the criminal litigation process.

Crime was once a rarity in the typical person's life. In late twentieth century America, it has become a pervasive social phenomenon, with nearly one in three households directly affected by a crime each year, and with more than one million convicted criminals currently behind bars. A person commits a crime by violating a criminal statute and, in this sense, criminal law is less judge-made than other branches of the common law. However, many criminal statutes essentially codify earlier, judge-made law. Moreover, all statutes are subject to judicial interpretation and review. Therefore, although criminal law is likely to be more diverse than most bodies of common law, making a unified account difficult, it is possible to identify key common institutional elements and to evaluate their impact on the efficiency of the law.

Let me begin by acknowledging the validity of a key assumption in economic analyses of crime, namely that the criminal mind is largely rational and that most crimes are deliberately committed for material (or at least for utilitarian) gain. This implies that changes in the expected cost of a crime, whether effected by changing the probability of apprehension and conviction or by changing the severity of the punishment, will have a perceptible impact upon the rate of criminal activity (*ceteris paribus*). An efficient criminal justice system will seek to minimize the joint cost of crime and punishment, not, of course, to eliminate crime entirely (Becker 1968). In so doing, it will not handicap itself by rules designated to make it difficult to apprehend and convict those who engage in criminal behavior. (Maas 1995 shows how rules of evidence handicapped the government in bringing its case against the master-spy Richard Ames in 1994).

This ideal is in no way descriptive of late twentieth century American criminal procedures, which are designed to make it exceptionally difficult and costly to convict the guilty and which place an unacceptably high value on ensuring that the innocent are not incorrectly convicted. It is my belief that almost all the institutional barriers erected against efficient criminal law procedures have their foundations in a deep-rooted skepticism about the ability of jurors to do their jobs (a skepticism which may be well-founded given the process of jury selection). In itself this constitutes a powerful argument in favor of the civil code procedure in which juries play no role.

The legal system is flawed, in the case of criminal law, from pretrial investigation to appeal. Indeed, in most criminal cases in the United States there is no trial. Police ineptitude is obvious, given the large budgets allocated to police departments and the fact that the overwhelming majority of all crimes go unsolved. If the police and prosecuting attorney become uncertain about their case, either they drop further investigation or the accused pleads guilty in return for a lower sentence. The defendant is formally charged in only a relatively few cases and trials occur in only a tiny fraction of crimes (Tullock 1996, 4–5).

Plea bargaining in itself is not necessarily an inefficient procedure. It need not deny the defendant the right to the procedural safeguards of a trial, nor need it lead, on average, to reduced sentences. If the trial procedure itself is efficient (which I suggest is not the case) plea bargains must be efficiency-enhancing since either party can elect to go to trial if they so prefer. Given a fixed prosecutorial budget, average sentences may actually increase where plea bargaining is allowed because the prosecutor can use resources saved by plea bargains to build stronger cases where such bargaining fails (Posner 1992, 562). Plea bargaining that occurs under the shadow of an inefficient criminal law system, however, is quite another story.

The law of evidence is at the root of this inefficiency, mired in the most procedurally complex set of rules in the Anglo-Saxon system. Many of the laws have evolved on the pretext (or reality) that jurors are simple people who are easily misled. Rightly or wrongly, the United States courts distrust juries. Many, if not most, of the exclusionary rules of evidence exclude evidence because judges consider that juries would be inclined to attach more weight to it than they ought (Rothstein 1970, 4–5). That is, judges believe that juries could not be trusted to give the evidence its logical, rational weight, or to perceive that it had none, but instead, perhaps because of the emotional impact of the evidence, would allow it to be more persuasive or influential than they should (Tullock 1996, 16–17).

Interestingly, judges are bound by the same rules of evidence as juries. Judges not infrequently review pieces of evidence to determine whether they have been submitted in violation of procedural rules. If they so find, they announce that they will not pay attention to such evidence in the proceedings. I doubt that many judges have the kind of mental discipline necessary to fulfill that kind of promise. In any event, judges are much less likely than juries to react emotionally to evidence currently excluded from consideration.

Many of the widely accepted ground rules that have become part of the criminal process following court decisions interpreting the fourth, fifth and sixth amendments of the Constitution allow obviously guilty and often violent criminals go free. The Supreme Court requires judges to advise jurors that no adverse inference may be drawn from the failure of a defendant to testify. It also requires judges to exclude illegally obtained evidence from criminal trials. The result of such rulings is a menaced society, unprotected by the legal system.

The laws of evidence encourage courts to reach erroneous outcomes because they are not allowed to take account of relevant evidence. From this perspective, it is possible to distinguish rules of evidence that are intended to benefit the accused, whether or not he is innocent, from rules of evidence that have no obvious bias, ruling out evidence for both the prosecution and the defense. The fifth amendment right not to testify against oneself and the *fruit of the poisonous tree* doctrine are prime examples of bias in favor of the accused. Other rules, as we shall see, change the procedure, but it is not obvious whether the defendant gains or loses.

The original meaning of the common law privilege against self-incrimination was simply that a person accused of a crime could not be called upon to testify. Indeed, in the early days in the colonies, not only could the accused not be called upon to testify, but it was illegal for him to testify on his own volition. The somewhat dubious privilege of not being permitted or compelled to testify was restricted to people who were accused of a crime. Other witnesses did not have this privilege.

The origins of this right to silence come from the sixteenth century maxim: "*nemo tenetur prodere se ipsum*" or, "no-one should be required to accuse himself." The right was applied haphazardly until the fifth amendment became law in 1791. For example, during the Salem witch trials of 1692, the judges believed that torture and death were appropriate persuasive techniques for recalcitrant defendants (Griswold 1955, Berger 1980).

The fifth amendment provides that no person shall be compelled in any criminal case to be witness against himself. The due process clause of the fourteenth amendment extends this privilege to state law. The privilege extends to civil proceedings if there is any threat of criminal sanctions associated with incriminating testimony. This privilege tends to be to the advantage of the accused. The defendant and his lawyer can weigh whether the former's testimony (and exposure to cross-examination) is more likely to benefit or to injure his case, given that the jury will note his failure to testify. Whether or not the judge should instruct the jury to ignore the defendant's failure to take the stand is itself a controversial question.

The fruit of the poisonous tree doctrine is biased in favor of the accused, at least *pro forma*. The doctrine prevents the prosecution from presenting evidence against a defendant when that evidence is the direct result or the immediate product of illegal conduct on the part of public officials responsible for extracting it. Examples of the application of this doctrine include the inadmissibility of evidence obtained from an illegal search and of confessions resulting from an illegal arrest.

The bias in favor of the defendant appears clear. However, the widespread publicity that the doctrine has received may actually bias the whole proceeding against the defendant. Jurymen may labor under the apprehension, based on newspaper and television accounts, that the prosecution typically is in possession of evidence which is barred because of this doctrine. If so, they may over-compensate for this perceived bias in their own deliberations, despite instructions from the bench.

Assume that the average juryman believes that fifteen per cent of the prosecution's case is prohibited by the laws of evidence. In some cases, the prosecution's case might be thirty per cent stronger and in others there might be no prohibited evidence. The jury correction factor, in such circumstances, would under-estimate the actual bias introduced by the laws of evidence in the former cases, and over-estimate it in the latter.

If the objective is accuracy, in the sense of an even bias, the poisonous tree doctrine is a clumsy way to try to achieve it. In the absence of a jury, the doctrine would be largely indefensible since professional judges would be fully capable of giving illegally obtained evidence an appropriate weighting. If society truly does not want illegal evidence to be obtained, it could devise appropriate penalties, including lengthy prison terms, for public officials who conspire to collect it, or who attempt to deploy it in the courtroom.

Let me now briefly comment on other rules of evidence that, in general, are quite impartial, in that they rule out evidence both for the prosecution and the defense, and yet reduce the information available to reach a correct verdict. The rule prohibiting hearsay evidence is a prime example of this genre.

It is clear that if a choice is available between hearing Mr. Smith testify about something that he saw or hearing Mr. Jones testify as to what Mr. Smith told him about what he saw, we would prefer the former to the latter evidence. The problem of "whispering down the lane" (Tullock 1965) suggests that information suffers from distortion as it is relayed from one person to another. Yet, if Mr. Smith is not available, then Mr. Jones' testimony may be better than nothing. That is the view taken by European courts, who would hear the hearsay evidence and discount its importance. In the United States, Mr. Jones' testimony would be inadmissible.

The hearsay rule does not necessarily protect the accused. Suppose that Mr. Smith was the only eye-witness to a murder and that he is now dead. Suppose that he had testified at a previous mistrial. It would seem that the jury is more likely to reach a correct verdict if Mr. Smith's evidence is admitted than if it is excluded. The point is highlighted if we further suppose that Mr. Smith's statement is the only evidence that can clear the accused of a murder charge, by providing the reasonable doubt necessary for an acquittal. Such considerations have no part in official doctrine, except to the formalistic extent that need and reliability are recognized in the exceptions to the hearsay rule. Yet, citizens, in making important decisions in their daily lives, rely extensively on their ability to correctly evaluate hearsay (Tullock 1996, 17–18).

The remaining rules of evidence are similar in their effect to the hearsay rule. If they have any justification at all, it is that they reduce the likelihood that unintelligent jurymen will be misled by poor or tainted evidence. To repeat my earlier assertion, if juries really are so suspect, why not remove them in favor of bench trials. Alternatively, one might take positive steps (such as requiring minimal intelligence quota levels) to improve the quality of the average jury. Of course, trial lawyers would lobby strongly against either reform since they have invested heavily in recent years in the techniques of jury manipulation.

Evaluating the effectiveness and efficiency of jury trials is a challenging process that is yet barely in its infancy. The fact that juries are instructed from the bench not to discuss the details of cases on which they have served indicates that proponents of the jury system are concerned about the likely public reaction, once information becomes available about what went on in the jury room. In recent years, jury members have begun to sell their stories to the gutter press and such stories do not reinforce the case for the jury system. In any event, a number of procedures have been devised to evaluate jury decision-making.

The classic study on the workings of the American jury was the 1966 report from the University of Chicago Law School (Kalven and Zeisel 1966). In this study, Kalven and Zeisel analyzed information on 3,576 criminal trials, having questioned 555 trial judges around the United States. The study used a measure of the rate and quality of judge-jury disagreements as a means of measuring jury efficiency. It determined that the judges who heard the cases would have reached different verdicts than the jury in thirty per cent of the cases studied. Disagreement was no more frequent in so-called "easy" cases than in "difficult" cases, a finding that Zeisel and Kalven inexplicably called: "a stunning refutation of the hypothesis that the jury does not understand."

According to the Chicago study, approximately twenty per cent of the judge-jury disagreement was due to juror sentiment about the law or about the defendant. Strong sentiment might even stimulate a juror to look for weaknesses in the facts or perhaps to nullify the law. As Zeisel and Kalven put it: "We know from other parts of our jury study that the jury does not often consciously and explicitly yield to sentiment in the truth of the law. Rather it yields to sentiment in the apparent process of resolving doubts as to evidence."

Disagreement between judge and jury also derives from other sources, as the Chicago study reported. One such source is the issue of witness credibility. Judges tend to be much more jaded about lying than juries. Another source of disagreement is that juries tend to have different standards than judges for *reasonable doubt*, tending to hold higher standards concerning how much proof overcomes the presumption of innocence in a criminal case. The difference is due, in part, to defense lawyers' rhetoric on the matter and in part to the greater degree of cynicism displayed by the bench. Of course, one cannot generalize about which judgment is superior. However, jury trials, from this perspective, bias cases in favor of the accused.

The Chicago study found that, when the judge and jury disagreed, it was usually in cases where the jury found in favor of the defendant. Factors that seem to have swayed the jury in such cases are: feelings of sympathy for the defendant; perceptions of police or prosecutorial abuse; attorney performance; and lack of information about the defendant's prior criminal record. The study could not conclude objectively whether the jury system was worth retaining. It did characterize the system as a: "daring effort in human arrangement to work out a solution to the tensions between law, equity and anarchy." Of course, many daring efforts have failed abysmally to achieve their objectives in the history of mankind. The jury system is one such failure.

Theoretically, the role of the jury is to decide the facts and to leave the law to the judge. Among those who actually deal with juries, there is virtually no one who believes that this theory accurately describes reality (Tullock 1996, 11). It is customary for the judge to give legal instructions to the jury to guide them in their decision-making processes. Evidence suggests that jurors typically forget some or all of these instructions and that they ignore instructions that they do not like. In an experimental jury exercise conducted by Hastie, Penrod and Pennington (1983) jury panelists were required to complete questionnaires, following their deliberations, which asked them about the judge's instructions on the law. Individual jurors performed only slightly better than random in their recall of the instructions.

There was a period in The People's Republic of China, initiated by Chairman Mao, when specialization of labor was jettisoned and individuals were encouraged to exchange occupations at will. Janitors periodically performed operations at hospitals under this dispensation (except, of course, when the secretary of the local communist party needed an operation). It is not in any way to be critical of these janitors to admit that they achieved an abnormally high death rate. As I shall suggest in *Chapter 6*, the error rate in American jury trials is at least one in eight. Although I do not wish to criticize Chinese janitors or American jurors as well-meaning individuals, the error term is always much higher when you use amateurs than when you use professionals (Tullock, 1980, 29).

Even the rare well-qualified jury labors under handicaps that the judge does not encounter, that extend well beyond the problems imposed by rules of evidence. For example, in some instances, rather than instructing the jury on the law, the law is deliberately withheld from the jury. This obfuscation is referred to as "blindfolding the jury." Juries usually are not informed about the consequences for criminal defendants that will follow from a verdict of not guilty by reason of insanity. Juries in comparative negligence jurisdictions usually are not informed as to when damages will be trebled or the effects of the attorneys' fees. Juries that are compelled to guess about such matters frequently guess incorrectly, compounding the weakness of the jury trial.

Juries are also handicapped, relative to the judge, with respect to the tools that they are permitted to use to assemble and to process the facts of the case. It is beyond rational logic to justify the prohibition imposed on United States juries from taking notes, reviewing evidence, asking questions and having access to basic information resources. Perhaps such prohibitions make judges feel superior. In the kingdom of the blind, the one-eyed man is king.

6. The Tragedie of the Common Law System in the United States

As I have noted earlier, Americans are much more litigious than other peoples. There are twenty times as many lawyers per capita in America as in Japan (a civil code country), five times as many as in Germany (also a civil code country) and four times as many as in England and Wales (a common law country). American trial courts disposed of more than four million civil cases in 1981, more than 2.5 million criminal cases and 0.6 million juvenile cases. In civil suits, contract cases dominated, producing about ten times as many trials as tort disputes, with property disputes somewhere in between. Some ninety-five per cent of all civil disputes are disposed of without resort to trial (Cooter and Ulen 1988, 478).

The social cost of legal disputes is unknown, but must be very high. In 1983, combined federal, state and local spending on civil and criminal justice amounted to $39.7 billion, or $170 per capita. This accounted for three per cent of all government spending in that year. Of this total, $37 per capita was expended on judicial services (Cooter and Ulen 1988, 478). This latter sum amounts to only a small fraction of the social cost of resolving disputes through the courts, since most of these costs are borne by private parties. In a back-of-the envelope calculation of the opportunity cost of all parties to a trial (based on a $20 per hour average cost), Cooter and Ulen (1981) estimated the labor cost of a full trial to be approximately $400 per hour, to which must be added the cost of court facilities. If this is even close to the mark, the costs showing up in government statistics represent only the tip of the iceberg of the total cost to society.

It is particularly instructive to compare litigation in the United States with that in England and Wales since both countries operate under the common law system. In part, the much lower rates of litigation in England and Wales occur because of cultural differences. Their citizens are much more inclined to take responsibility for their own misfortunes, much less inclined to seek socialized protection from risk through the court system than are United States citizens. This greater independence of spirit is reinforced by institutional factors that make litigation less attractive.

In England and Wales, the loser of a lawsuit must pay the litigation costs of the winner, whereas in the United States each party ordinarily pays his own litigation costs. Given risk aversion, this reduces the volume of litigation. In England and Wales, contingency fees are prohibited. This reduces the incentives for lawyers to ambulance-chase and to pressure reluctant parties into litigating for damages that truly have not been sustained, behavior that has become a pronounced feature of American trial lawyers since the 1960's. In England and Wales, all civil trials are bench trials, significantly reducing the cost of litigation and avoiding entirely the ridiculously high awards culled out of carefully selected U.S. juries by emotive trial lawyer rhetoric. In England and Wales, ethnic and race diversity does not give rise to the kind of jury tensions that lead to so many hung juries in the United States with associated high litigation costs in criminal suits. In England and Wales, the law of contract has not been destroyed by the law of tort as has occurred in certain states in America, notably California, again under sustained pressure from the Association of Trial Lawyers of America.

If litigation costs indeed are so high in the United States, does this imply that high degrees of accuracy are achieved by the U.S. courts, that truth is better served in America than elsewhere? Such evidence as is available does not support this proposition.

Errors can occur either in interpreting the law or in matters of fact (Tullock 1994, 9). Let me first address errors of fact. Under the common law system, court decisions actually make a good deal of the law, and hence the meaning of error is more ambiguous, though, as I shall demonstrate, error can be identified as unacceptable deviations from precedent and stare decisis. Again, let me focus primarily on the criminal law to address the issue of errors of fact.

Suppose that a prominent socialite is brutally murdered and that following a police investigation, her ex-husband is the prime suspect, albeit on the basis of circumstantial evidence. The court does not know whether or not he is guilty. It simply knows how much evidence there is against him. There are various rules that the court can use and I shall canvass a number of them, starting with the rule now used in civil suits, not criminal, namely take whichever is the most probable result. This minimizes total errors, type 1 and type 2. The guilty ex-husband has a three out of four chance of being convicted and a one out of four chance of being acquitted. The innocent ex-husband has a three out of four chance of being discharged and a one out of four chance of being convicted in my model (Tullock 1984).

To deter the crime under this rule, assuming risk neutral criminals, a penalty levied at 1.334 times the benefit to the criminal is minimally required. The innocent ex-husband has a present discounted penalty, again assuming risk neutrality, of one-third the benefit from the crime.

The normal rule in criminal law, however, is that the defendant will be convicted only if the evidence against him is *beyond all reasonable doubt*. Assume that the weight of evidence required for conviction gives a probability of eighty per cent or higher of guilt. Under these circumstances, according to my model, thirty-six per cent of guilty persons and four per cent of innocent persons will be convicted (Tullock 1992, 11).

To deter the crime under this rule, assuming universal risk neutrality, a penalty levied at 2.777 times the benefit to the criminal must be imposed. The present discounted cost to the innocent of such a penalty is a little over ten per cent of the assessed benefit from the crime. Although the expected cost to the innocent is lower under the criminal law standard, it is not as low as would be the case if the total magnitude of the penalty need not be increased to compensate for the lowered probability that the guilty will escape punishment. Errors with respect to the facts predictably are greater in criminal lawsuits than in civil lawsuits simply because an inefficient burden of proof is required.

One method of measuring the error rate of courts is to compare the verdicts of two independent decision-making bodies. If the two bodies disagree about a given case, one of them must be wrong. If they are in agreement, it is possible that both are wrong. A measure of court error rates based on disagreement thus provides a minimum value (Tullock 1980, 32). Two studies (one in the United States, the other in England) independently confirm that the error rate of courts is approximately one in eight.

The first such study is the 1966 report from the University of Chicago Law School by Kalven and Zeisel (discussed in more detail in *Chapter 5*). In a response rate to questionnaires, in excess of 3,500 judges were asked to mark down their own verdicts against the jury verdicts. Disagreements occurred in one-fourth of the cases. There is no way of telling from this data whether it is the judge or the jury which is in error, though the professional qualifications of the judge, in my view, generally ensure that his error rate will be the lower. In a more recent study in England by Baldwin and McConnville (1979), based on similar methodology, an error rate somewhat in excess of one in eight was reported.

Of course, no system, legal or otherwise, is entirely immune from error, and there is no obvious way of determining what the optimal error rate should be. However, if a lower cost method results in a lower average error rate surely there should be a cost-effective presumption in favor of that method. In my view, that presumption conclusively favors a switch away from jury trials to bench trials, whether or not the common law itself is jettisoned in favor of the civil code. Recognition of court error could influence the choice among legal rules and legal remedies. This is a factor that almost universally is ignored in the law and economics literature (Tullock 1980, 48).

Perhaps the strongest argument in favor of courts rather than legislators as lawmakers is that advanced by Bruno Leoni, an Italian lawyer trained in the Italian civil code tradition. In his book, *Freedom and the Law* (1961), Leoni noted that the bulk of Roman law had been created by *juris consults*, who, if they were not actually judges, nevertheless had developed a common law from the consideration of real cases. A judgment did not become a true precedent until it had been reached independently in separate cases by several judges. In Roman law, there was no truly binding supreme court decision, although individual cases rarely might be appealed to the senate or to the emperor. Hence, the need for a sequence of confirmatory judgments.

Until 1800, the same was essentially true of the English common law system. Prior to the Benthamite reform movement, the British government is best described as an institution like Topsy that "just growed" without conscious design. The English common law itself had evolved out of a competing court system and was composed of judgments that had survived repeated scrutiny. Appeals to the House of Lords, though theoretically possible, were rare events. This implied that the common law evolved only very slowly and that changes had to survive a sequence of independent judgments before becoming established as precedent and subject to *stare decisis*.

Unfortunately for the common law system in America, the Founding Fathers were impatient with the apparent untidiness of a slowly evolving system. They hankered for a court of last resort which could make binding rulings and hence tidy up the common law. The result was the Supreme Court which gradually has abandoned its role as constitutional guardian in favor of a more glamorous, if dangerous, role as law-maker. Instead of common law changes slowly evolving by surviving repeated independent scrutiny, a single simple majority ruling of the Supreme Court now changes the law instantly, in some cases to an extreme degree. Needless to say, the Supreme Court does not consider itself to be bound by its own previous judgments.

The weakness of the Supreme Court in responding to special interest group pressure has not been lost on the lower courts, both federal and state, as is evidenced by the almost complete abandonment of classical civil law principles and by the growing rush to protect the guilty through changes in criminal law procedures. Even the unambiguous wording of the Constitution has not been allowed to impede this misguided law-making impulse. Let me briefly illustrate by listing some of the more egregious changes in the law of property, contract and tort.

One of the most serious invasions of the law of property was the unlawful judgment of the Supreme Court in *Penn Central Transportation Co. v. City of New York* (1978). The court, speaking through Justice Brennan, held that the state may exclude persons from the occupation occupation of part of what they own and still not come under a prima facie obligation to pay compensation. This judgment set the pace for a decade of unconstitutional judgments which, for a time at least, effectively eliminated the fifth amendment protection against the seizure of private property by government for public use without the payment of just compensation.

Although there has been an uneven drift back towards constitutionality on this issue since 1988, the Supreme Court remains a less than effective defender of fifth amendment rights (Rowley 1992, 121–122). Given this example by the Supreme Court, it is not surprising that lower courts have also abandoned the defense of property rights, for example, determining disputes over property by reference to least cost avoider considerations rather than by recognition of the inalienable right to property (Barnes and Stout 1992, Chap 2). Legal rules that do not effectively protect property rights render individuals vulnerable to coercion by others and reduce wealth to society.

In the most famous passages in economics, Adam Smith (1776) set out the justification for what is now referred to as the classical law of contract:

> "It is not from the benevolence of the butcher, the brewer, or the baker that we expect our dinner, but from their regard to their own interest. We address ourselves, not to their humanity, but to their self-love; and never talk to them of their own necessities, but of their advantages... Every individual is continually exerting himself to find out the most advantageous employment for whatever capital he can command. It is his own advantage, indeed, and not that of society, which he has in view. But the study of his own advantage, naturally, or rather necessarily, leads him to prefer that employment which is most advantageous to society... He is in this... led by an invisible hand to promote an end which was no part of his intention. Nor is it always the worse for society that it was no part of it. By pursuing his own interest, he frequently promotes that of society more effectively than when he really intends to promote it." (Smith 1776, 14, 421, 423).

In this view, the public interest is furthered as a mere by-product of countless self-serving individual decisions to engage in trade or exchange. The legal counterpart to this view of the market is the *will* or *autonomy* theory of contract law, where obligations by individuals to one another arise out of voluntarily assumed, self-imposed obligations reflecting convergent intentions of the contracting parties (Trebilcock 1993, 241). The classical law of contract, in its heyday, was viewed as simultaneously promoting autonomy (or individual freedom) and social welfare. In the United States, the courts have retreated dramatically from the classical position, *stare decisis* notwithstanding, under a combination of special interest group pressures and socialist ideology.

Under classical contract law all that was required for a binding contract was offer, acceptance and consideration since the courts would not inquire into the latter's adequacy. Absent any one of these a contract would not be upheld at law. Now, courts read in consideration when it is not there, in order to uphold promises that individuals relied upon when they should not have done so. They strike down bargains that should be upheld simply because some judge does not like the terms the parties agreed to.

Courts strike down bargains on the ground of incomplete information, ignoring the fact that the future is always uncertain. They strike down bargains on the ground of cognitive deficiencies on the part of one party or the other, ignoring the fact that talent is unevenly distributed across human beings. They strike down contracts on the ground that they contain terms that are "unconscionable" or "contrary to public policy" again as viewed by some judge, not by the parties to the bargain (Barnes and Stout 1992, Chap. 4). Most damaging of all, they strike down bargains on the grounds that they contain third party effects, ignoring the fact that externalities are universal and that the very large majority of them are not Pareto-relevant (Peacock and Rowley 1975). In this way, U.S. courts have allowed the law of tort to emasculate the law of contract with very serious consequences for individual autonomy and for the wealth of the nation.

Until the 1950's, the tradition with respect to the law of accidents and personal injury was to concentrate the attention of the courts on civil wrongs involving strangers, where contracts could not govern the relationships between the parties. The line between contract and tort tended to be tightly drawn, in favor of contract to the maximum extent possible. For a tort case to succeed under classical common law, there had to be a breach of a duty owed to the plaintiff by the defendant, harm suffered by the plaintiff and proximate cause. In such circumstances, the negligence with contributory negligence standard typically was applied. Damages were narrowly construed, essentially to replace medical costs and loss of earnings.

From the early 1960's, however, the U.S. courts systematically assaulted the classical law of tort dismantling its twin historic pillars—deterrence and compensation—in favor of notions of societal insurance and risk-spreading and undermining the concept of fault as a doctrinal mechanism for limiting tort liability to substantive tortfeasors (Huber 1988, Rowley 1989). The abandonment of proximate cause in favor of joint and several liability has fired the engines of the rent-seekers who now specifically target the deep pockets. The shift from negligence with contributory negligence to comparative negligence or strict liability standards has induced a sharp increase in moral hazard as plaintiffs lower their own standards of care and has stimulated a sharp increase in tertiary legal costs as the volume of law suits has exploded. The widening of damages to encompass pain and suffering and loss of companionship damages as well as to anticipate harms that have not even occurred has made a mockery of the law and has eliminated a wide range of otherwise viable goods and services from the American market-place (Barnes and Stout 1992, chap. 3).

In no sense is this retreat from classical tort law and the emasculation of contract law to be viewed as a slow evolutionary process. Rather it is the product of rent-seeking trial lawyers, activist judges and gullible juries who together have conspired to shackle capitalism into the confines of the plantation state (Jasay 1980). So diseased has the US common law system become that even root-and-branch internal reform no longer is feasible. If individual autonomy and the rule of law is to be re-established, Wellington must now cede victory to Napoleon and the common law must give way to the civil code.

7. Why I Prefer Napoleon

My principal purpose in this monograph is to outline the case against the common law, not to set out a detailed case in favor of the civil law. The latter task is better suited to a specialist in civil code procedures, more experienced than I am in the detailed workings of the civil code in the Western European democracies. Although I personally prefer the Napoleonic code to Anglo-Saxon procedures, for reasons that I shall set out in this Chapter, I do not think that it is in any sense ideal. Whether or not Napoleon was right and Blackstone wrong will be answered definitively only if the whole discussion is opened up to scientific investigation. Readers, therefore, may wish to treat my assertions in this chapter as testable hypotheses. They may even wish to take time out to test them, by engaging in the kind of comparative institutions analysis which is sorely lacking in this field.

Let me start by outlining the case advanced in favor of the common law system by its most fervent contemporary advocate, Judge Richard Posner (Posner 1992). By countering that case point by point, and by drawing upon additional arguments outlined earlier in this monograph, I shall advance my own case for adopting some variant of the Napoleonic code.

For Posner (1992), the ultimate question for decision in many lawsuits is what allocation of resources would maximize efficiency. The market normally decides this question, but it is given to the legal system to decide in situations where the cost of a market determination would exceed those of a legal determination. Like the market, the common law uses prices equal to opportunity costs to induce people to maximize efficiency. Where compensatory damages are the remedy for a breach of legal duty, the effect of liability is not to compel compliance with law but to compel the violator to pay a price equal to the opportunity costs of the violation. Although heavier sanctions—penalties—are sometimes imposed, normally this is done in circumstances where penalties are necessary to create the correct economic activities.

Again, according to Posner (1992), the legal process, like the market, relies for its administration primarily on private individuals motivated by economic self-interest rather than on altruists or public officials. Through the lawyer that he hires, the victim of conduct that may be unlawful in a civil case: (1) investigates the circumstances surrounding the allegedly unlawful act; (2) organizes the information obtained by the investigation; (3) decides whether to activate the machinery of legal allocation; (4) feeds information in a digestible form to that machinery; (5) checks the accuracy of the information supplied by the defendant; (6) presses if necessary for changes in the rules of allocation followed by the courts; and (7) sees to the collection of the judgment.

As opposed to criminal law, because of this private activity, the state can dispense with a police force to protect people's common law rights, public attorneys to enforce them and other bureaucratic personnel to operate the system. Such functionaries would be less highly motivated than a private plaintiff since their economic self-interest would be affected only indirectly by the outcomes of particular cases.

The legal process (again according to Posner 1992) also resembles the market in its impersonality, most particularly in its subordination of distributive considerations. The invisible hand of the market has its counterpart in the disinterest of the judge. The method by which judges are compensated and the rules of judicial ethics are designed to ensure that the judge will have no financial or other interest in the outcome of a case before him, no responsibility other than to decide issues tendered by the parties and no knowledge of the facts in the case other than what the competition of the parties conveys to him. Jurors are similarly constrained.

In his zeal to liken the common law system to a private market, Posner oversteps the mark. The common law system is not a private market place. It is a socialistic bureaucracy in which attorneys essentially lobby government officials—judges and juries—much in the same way that special interest groups lobby the legislature. The greater the rents at stake in an action, the more lavish will be the outlay of resources on attorney-lobbyists and on expert witness-lobbyists whose prime goal is to tilt the judgment of the judge-jury regulators in favor of their client. In some cases, attorneys will engage in judge-shopping to secure a compliant judge and in jury manipulation to secure a compliant jury. The distinction between the common law courthouse and the legislature is far less than Posner is willing to admit.

Posner is correct in asserting that the common law system economizes in the use of judges and other public officials, by substituting the private activity of the parties for the information collecting responsibility of bureaucrats. The ratio of judges to lawyers well may be ten times higher in Sweden and in Germany than in California, as Posner (1992) suggests. However, as Posner fails to note, that ratio is made up of a denominator as well as a numerator. Civil law countries resolve their legal business with between one-tenth and one-twentieth the number of practising lawyers as the U.S., and without any significant recourse to juries. The common law is an extremely high cost legal system by comparison with all civil code alternatives. Posner is silent on this issue, which is central to the debate, despite the fact that he relies extensively on transaction cost evidence in all other areas of his economic analysis of law.

To the extent that the common law relies on compensatory damages as the remedy for a breach of legal duty, it does make use of price as a mechanism to rectify market failure. However, as I indicate in *Chapter 6*, juries are extremely inefficient mechanisms for calculating compensatory damages and are prone to emotive responses to carefully targeted attorney rhetoric; responses that result in grossly excessive damage awards. If many of those awards are reduced subsequently on appeal, this is at additional legal cost and induced by a mechanism much closer to civil code procedure in that it makes no use of juries and strictly limits attorney advocacy, at least with respect to the facts of the case.

As I have argued in *Chapters 4* and *5*, the invisible hand of the market does not have its counterpart in the disinterest of the judge. Rather, its counterpart is the visible boot of the politically active judge and the bony knees and elbows of the semi-blindfold, intellectually lame jury. Competition between the parties does not convey information efficiently to the courtroom because laws of evidence are designed deliberately to obfuscate the process. In consequence, the American legal system at best is extremely capricious and at worst is a random lottery. It would be much more cost-effective, in such circumstances, to decide outcomes by flipping a coin or by rolling a dice rather than by indulging in the high cost farce of the typical jury trial.

There are three basic differences between the Anglo-Saxon common law system and the Napoleonic civil law system on which I shall focus attention in this concluding section namely: (1) the accusatorial versus the inquisitorial method of procedure, (2) the presence versus the absence of the jury and (3) laws that limit versus laws that require full disclosure of the evidence. With respect to each of these differences, it is my contention that the Napoleonic system is superior to the common law system (Tullock 1988).

The Anglo-Saxon adversarial process is utilized only in common law countries. The majority of countries, those that adhere to civil code procedures, utilize the inquisitorial system, whereby the judge (or magistrate) takes the lead in gathering evidence and forming the issues of a case. In such a system, lawyers have a subordinate role, much less than principal players in the litigation process.

In criminal cases, the police investigate so that a prosecutor can decide whether to proceed or to drop a case. The police have two different types of power, depending on whether the case is an ordinary investigation (*enquete preliminaire*) or a flagrant offense (*enquete flagrante*). A flagrant offense is a serious crime which can be punished by imprisonment or a crime which is currently being committed. The police have more extensive powers to preserve evidence in such cases than in ordinary investigations. There are no search and seizure requirements or restrictions other than rules designed to guarantee individual rights. Once the police hand over the investigation to the prosecutor, the accused is charged or the case is dismissed.

Once the decision to prosecute has been made, the detection apparatus and the court system combine under the authority of a legally trained judicial official or magistrate. This official conducts an investigation personally if it is a serious crime or supervises the investigation if the crime is less complex. The police are available to assist the official with his inquiries. The official typically inspects the scene of the crime, conducts examinations and searches, questions all persons possibly associated with the crime, and allows witnesses to confront each other.

The suspect is involved throughout the process of gathering evidence and constructing the case. He can make representations to the official and argue his point of view. He may choose to be represented by an attorney at this stage. The suspect is interrogated (no, not with rubber hoses as many U.S. attorneys characteristically believe) to try to extract a confession. The focus of the investigation is to discharge a falsely suspected person and there is (again contrary to U.S. attorney beliefs) a presumption of innocence. All of these proceedings are recorded in a dossier which is presented to the judges if the case goes to trial.

Magistrates formally decide the accused's guilt or innocence. If the accused is found guilty there is a trial, normally before a bench of three, typically composed of one judge and two assessors. Committal to trial under the civil code system is more probative because the suspect has participated in all the inquiries whereas only the police side is presented in a U.S. preliminary hearing. The trial itself, to some extent, is an appeal from the initial judicial proceeding (Hanson 1955, 272).

Once the criminal case is ready for trial the procedure becomes somewhat more accusatorial, though the bench is much less influenced by lawyers' courtroom strategies under the inquisitorial system. When the trial is completed the panel retires to its chamber and reaches a decision by simple majority vote. The assessors can outvote the judge on issues of fact, though they usually defer to his judgment on matters of law (Tullock 1980, 11). European courts generally apply the maxim: "if there is doubt, acquit." Generally, under the civil system, a defendant who confesses and repents has his sentence reduced by twenty-five per cent.

The civil code tribunals admit almost any evidence provided that it is relevant to the case, and then let the judges decide whether it is good or bad and how much weight to attach to it. Evidence is presented which would be barred under the Anglo-Saxon system. For example, hearsay is admitted but given less weight than direct testimony. The defendant can be sworn in and questioned by the judge. The defendant can refuse to answer questions but the judge will take any such refusal into account. There is no fifth amendment privilege.

The judges can ask for whatever evidence they want and do not have to listen to evidence that they do not want. The President, or chief judge, decides the order in which witnesses are called and can ask questions of the witness. The bench has full access to the detailed record of evidence compiled by the magistrate. The accused may be tried *in absentia*. Judgments tend to be much better informed in civil code than in common law trials. They are also rendered by well-trained professionals and not by ignorant amateurs.

Appeals can be made from the judgment of the initial court of decision. The typical European courts acknowledge that local courts can make errors both of fact and of law and hear both categories of appeal. European Supreme Courts also have a wider basis of jurisdiction than the U.S. Supreme Court. For example, a legislator or other official can ask for a European Supreme court's opinion on constitutional issues without awaiting a real legal dispute. In the United States, this is not possible (Tullock 1980, 37–38).

The code originally set up by Emperor Napoleon drew its inspiration from the laws introduced by the Emperor Justinian in Ancient Rome and from the laws of the mercantile town of Lombardy in Italy. The code replaced the orders of the king and his courts with a concise body of rules and principles. A representative body of the people was empowered with law-making functions, and developed the rules and principles still used today. Laws of procedure are not allowed to obstruct rules of substance. European code-based law is much briefer and much less ambiguous than Anglo-Saxon legislative laws.

Initially, the code made use of the jury for criminal cases. Over time, however, most continental Western European countries abandoned the jury system, leaving only a few remnants and these were exclusively for criminal trials. For example, murder cases in Switzerland are tried by a fifteen-man jury. In France, the *cour d'assises* (Court of Assize) is a criminal court which utilizes a jury. There is a professional judge accompanied by two assessors and a nine-man jury. Together, they deliberate and decide questions of law and fact, the guilt or otherwise of the accused and the appropriate sentence. A guilty verdict must be approved by a qualified majority of at least eight to four votes. If five votes are in favor of the accused, he is either acquitted or granted extenuating circumstances according to the principle of *minorite de faveur* (favorable minority). The sentencing decision must be supported by at least seven votes (eight in the case of custodial sentences or *peine privative de liberte*).

The European procedures are far superior in clarity, precision and implementation to the United States common law procedures. They lead to more accurate verdicts at a significantly lower cost. Essentially, the United States clings to an inefficient legal system which developed in the Middle Ages without much thought and which has evolved across the centuries without serious examination into whether or not its basic premises are sound. Its survival is due in part to tradition and in part because it guarantees large incomes to many of those connected with it.

Evidence in support of my judgment is available from recent experience in the United States where parties increasingly contract out of the American court system committing themselves instead to arbitration. Most commonly, arbitration takes the form of a summary inquisitorial process. Lawyers are banned, juries are not part of the process and expert witnesses are not called. Arbitrators are selected on the basis of their professional knowledge and their independence from the parties. Usually they do not write detailed opinions supporting their verdict.

Arbitration appears to be well-liked by those with the foresight to avoid the U.S. court system. In areas where it is applicable, it is set fair to supersede the common law system, introducing a private code system by default. The success of the inquisitorial arbitration system provides an ongoing challenge to those of my colleagues who continue stubbornly to defend an antiquated high cost legal system. Like King Canute, they may order the tides to change direction. Like King Canute, their orders will be swept aside by the powerful tides of economic efficiency. By design or by default, Napoleon will defeat Wellington on this important battlefield.

References

Baldwin, J. and McConnville, M. (1979). *Jury Trials.* Oxford: The Clarendon Press.

Becker, G.S. (1968). "Crime and Punishment: An Economic Approach." *Journal of Political Economy* 76.

Barnes, D.W. and Stout, L.A. (1992). *Cases and Materials on Law and Economics.* St. Paul: West Publishing Co.

Benson, B.L. (1990). *The Enterprise of Law.* San Francisco: Pacific Research Institute for Public Policy.

Berger, M. (1980). *Taking the 5th.* New York: Lexington Books.

Blackstone, W. (1973). *Commentaries on the Laws of England.* London: Macmillan.

Brough, W. and Kimenyi, M.S. (1987). *"Rites of Passage: The Bar Examination as Central Enforcement Mechanism."* Washington, D.C.: Legal Services Corporation.

Coase, R.H. (1960). "The Problem of Social Cost." *Journal of Law and Economics* III, 1-44.

Cooter, R. and Kornhauser (1980). "Can Litigation Improve the Law Without the Help of Judges?" *Journal of Legal Studies* IX, 139-63.

Cooter, R. and Ulen, T. (1988). *Law and Economics.* Glenview: Scott, Foresman & Company.

Dadomo, C. and Farran, S. (1987). *The French Legal System.* London: Sweet & Maxwell.

Dicey, A.V. (1987). *Introduction to the Law of the Constitution.* London: Macmillan.

DiPerma, P. (1984). *Juries on Trial: Faces of American Justice.* New York: Dembner Books.

Eisenberg, M.A. (1988). *The Nature of the Common Law.* Cambridge: Harvard University Press.

Ferguson, R.J. and Miller, A.L. (1974). *Polygraph for the Defense.* New York: Thomas Books.

Goetz, C.J. (1987). "Public Choice and the Law: The Paradox of Tullock" in C.K. Rowley (Ed.) *Democracy and Public Choice*. Oxford: Basil Blackwell 171-180.

Good, I.J. and Tullock, G. (1984). "Judicial Errors and a Proposal for Reform." *Journal of Legal Studies* XIII (2), 289-298.

Griswold, E.H. (1955). *The Fifth Amendment Today*. Cambridge: Harvard University Press.

Hanson, C.J. (1955). "The Prosecution of the Accused." *Criminal Law Review*.

Hastie, R., Penrod, S. and Pennington, N. (1983). *Inside the Jury*. Cambridge: Harvard University Press.

Hayek, F.A. (1983). *Law, Legislation and Liberty*, Volume I. London: Routledge & Kegan Paul.

Higgins, R.S. and Rubin, P.H. (1980). "Judicial Discretion" *Journal of Legal Studies* IX, 129-139.

Hogue, A. (1985). *Origins of the Common Law*. Indianapolis: Liberty Press.

Huber, P.W. (1988). *Liability: The Legal Revolution and its Consequences*. New York: Basic Books.

Jasay, A de (1980). *The State*. Oxford: Basil Blackwell.

Kalven, H. (1964). The Dignity of the Civil Jury. *Virginia Law Review*, 50.

Kalven, H. and Zeisel, H. (1966). *The American Jury*. Boston: Little, Brown & Co.

Kimenyi, M.S., Shughart, W.F. and Tollison, R.D. (1985). "What Do Judges Maximize?" *Journal of Public Finance and Public Choice* 3.

Leoni, B. (1961). *Freedom and the Law*. Los Angeles: Nash Publishing.

Locke, J. (1991). *Two Treatises of Government*. New York: Cambridge University Press.

Maas, P. (1995). *Killer Spy*. New York: Time Warner.

Maurizi, A. (1974). "Occupational Licensing and the Public Interest." *Journal of Political Economy* 82, 399-413.

McCabe, S. and Purves, R. (1972). *The Jury at Work*. London: Basil Blackwell Publishers.

McCormick, R, and Tollison, R.D. (1981). *Politicians, Legislation and the Economy*. Boston: Martinus Nighoff Publishing.

Posner, R.A. (1985). *The Federal Courts: Crisis and Reform.* Cambridge: Harvard University Press.

Posner, R.A. (1990). *The Problems of Jurisprudence.* Cambridge: Harvard University Press.

Posner, R.A. (1992). *Economic Analysis of the Law,* Fourth Edition. Boston: Little, Brown & Co.

Posner, R.A. (1993) What Do Judges Maximize. *Supreme Court Economic Review* 23.

Posner, R.A. (1995) *Overcoming Law.* Cambridge: Harvard University Press.

Priest, G.L. and Klein, B. (1984). "The Selection of Disputes for Litigation." *Journal of Legal Studies* XIII (1).

Rothstein, P.F. (1970). *Evidence in a Nutshell.* St Paul: West Publishing Co.

Rothwax, H.J. (1996). *The Collapse of Criminal Justice.* New York: Random House.

Rowley, C.K. and Peacock, A.T. (1975). *Welfare Economics: A Liberal Restatement.* Oxford: Martin Robertson.

Rowley, C.K. (1989). "The Common Law in Public Choice Perspective." *Hamline Law Review,* 12(2), 355-383.

Rowley, C.K. (1992). *The Right to Justice.* Aldershot: Edward Elgar Publishing.

Rowley, C.K. (1992). "The Supreme Court and Takings Judgments." in N. Mercuro (Ed.). *Taking Property and Just Compensation.* Boston: Kluwer Academic Publishers.

Rowley, C.K., Shughart, W.F. and Tollison, R.D. (1987). "Interest Groups and Deficits," in J.M. Buchanan, C.K. Rowley and G. Tullock (Eds.). *Deficits.* Oxford: Basil Blackwell.

Rubin, P.H. (1977). "Why is the Common Law Efficient?" *Journal of Legal Studies* 51-63.

Smith, A. (1991). *The Wealth of Nations,* Norwalk: Easton Press.

Spooner, L. (1852). *An Essay on Trial by Jury.*

Trebilock, M.J. (1993). *The Limits of Freedom of Contract.* Cambridge: Harvard University Press.

Tullock, G. (1965). *The Politics of Bureaucracy.* Washington, DC: Public Affairs Press.

Tullock, G. (1967). "The Welfare Cost of Tariffs, Monopolies and Theft." *Western Economic Journal* 5, 224-232.

Tullock, G. (1969). "An Economic Approach to Crime." *Social Science Quarterly* 50, 59-71.

Tullock, G. (1971). *The Logic of the Law.* New York: Basic Books.

Tullock, G. and Schwartz, W.F. (1975). "The Costs of a Legal System." *Journal of Legal Studies* 4, 75-82.

Tullock, G. (1980). Trials on Trial: The Pure Theory of Legal Procedure. New York: Columbia University Press.

Tullock, G. (1984). "Judicial Errors and a Proposal for Reform" *Journal of Legal Studies*, XIII, No. 4 (June): 289-98.

Tullock, G. (1987). "Negotiated Settlements" in G. Skogh and M. Schulenburg (Eds). *Law and Economics and the Economics of Legal Regulation.* Boston: Kluwer Academic Publishers.

Tullock, G. (1988). "Defending the Napoleonic Code over the Common Law" in S.S. Nagel (ed.) *Research in Law and Policy Studies* No. 2. New York: JAI Press.

Tullock, G. (1990). *Trials on Trials Revisited.* Tucson: University of Arizona Working Paper.

Tullock, G. (1993) *Rent-Seeking.* Shaftesbury Paper 3. Aldershot: Edward Elgar Publishing.

Tullock, G. (1994). "Court Errors." *European Journal of Law and Economics* 1, 9-21.

Tullock, G. (1995a). "Rent-Seeking and the Law" in J. Casas-Pardo and F. Schneider (Eds.) *Current Issues in Public Choice.* Aldershot: Edward Elgar Publishing.

Tullock, G. (1995b). "On the Desirable Degree of Detail in the Law." *European Journal of Law and Economics* Vol. 1.

Tullock, G. (1996). "Legal Heresy" *Economic Inquiry* Vol. XXXIV No. 1, 1-9.

Table of Cases

Index

voir dire, 30
vote, 22, 27–28, 57
    majority, 3, 20–22, 27, 29, 31,
        38, 49, 51, 56–57, 59
    voter, 31

Wales, 20, 45–46
War of Revolution, 7, 29
waste, social, 26
wealth maximization, 35

wealth transfer, 14
Wellington, 52, 59
West Coast Hotel v. Parrish, 19
Western Europe, 5
Williams v. Florida, 30
witness, 26, 33–34, 40, 43, 58
    expert, 33, 55, 59
writ, 8

Zeisel, H, 42–43, 48